Digital World – Analogue Church

Rebalancing technology in corporate worship

David M Snelling

ISBN: 1511468491
ISBN-13: 978-1511468497

CONTENTS

PREFACE

This is a book of questions. Some of which I seek to answer, some of which are left for you to ponder. In no way do I seek to be anti-technological in what I have written – that would be rather hypocritical of me given the amount of electronics I use to make music. What I seek to achieve with this book is to raise awareness of the issues of technology that have crept into our corporate worship, perhaps without us even noticing.

To that end, the first half of this book seeks to address wider themes of the nature of technology and its role within music. Consequently, it may appear at first glance that this book is more sociological than theological. However, having established some of the common problems that arise within technological forms, the second half of the book will seek to explain how this impacts our church life and finally will try and find ways of keeping the technological world in check.

The two churches that are described at the start of this book are entirely fictional and simply exist to provide a point of reference for the final chapter where we return to see how, in the light of knowledge gained in the prior discussions, we can bring technology into balance within their corporate worship life.

If, as a consequence of reading this book, you are led to question the place of the technological in church life and how it affects our theology, then I will consider it a success.

David M Snelling
Westbury, June 2015

ACKNOWLEDGMENTS

My thanks go to those who have supported and encouraged me through the production of this book. First of all, a big thank you to the staff, faculty and students of the *London School of Theology* where the seed of the idea for this project was first planted. Also to the members of WEC International's *Resonance* multicultural arts ministry, with whom I have worked since 2011, for the many conversations we have had about the nature and practice of corporate worship. Thanks, as well, to the congregations of Trinity URC in Harrow, Ryde Baptist Church on the Isle of Wight and West End Baptist Church in Westbury, who have supported me in my worship ministry and have been unwitting guinea pigs for some of the ideas presented here.

I am enormously grateful to Naomi Bignell and Esther McManus for reading through the draft manuscript and offering their constructive criticism, and last, but in no way least, to my wife, Jean, for her seemingly never-ending store of patience as she consistently pushed me on when the procrastination gene kicked in.

Any mistakes are entirely mine.

The front cover image shows the interior of La Sainte-Chapelle in Paris and was taken by Trey Ratcliff (also known as StuckInCustoms). More of his brilliant work can be found at flickr.com. The cover photo has been reproduced under a Creative Commons licence.

INTRODUCTION

Imagine, if you would, two churches.[1] The first is a small chapel set in a commuter belt. Once at the heart of a vibrant community, the glory days for this place are over. They have an ageing congregation of around 40 people. There are one or two families in attendance, but no children's or youth work to speak of, nor the personnel to maintain it if they did. They use a hymnbook for their music and an old upright piano that has really seen better days. Their minister is nearing retirement and, due to the fact that most of the congregation are retired themselves, there is little prospect of being able to pay for his successor. They have already had to sell off the vicarage, and most of the money in the offering plate goes towards the maintenance of their historic building. Although any visitors that join them are warmly welcomed, they rarely return. The congregation are faithful worshipers week-by-week, but after the morning service, the doors are closed until the following Sunday. They have tried to stage some events in the past, but they have always been poorly attended and it's a real struggle to find willing volunteers to run them. There is a small prayer group that meets on a Wednesday lunchtime to pray for their community, but it is only attended by three or four people at the most. They have a sincere, loving faith and long for someone to come and turn their fortunes around, but the vultures are circling and if that someone doesn't arrive soon, this church will be gone within a decade.

Travel a few miles down the road to a local industrial estate. Here is a church that meets in a warehouse building. Every Sunday, a dedicated team of volunteers arrives to

---

[1] These churches are fictitious. Any resemblance to actual congregations is entirely coincidental.

put out chairs and set up their portable stage and audio-visual systems. A great deal of effort goes into making this dark, utilitarian building a suitable space for Christian worship. Coloured lights whirl around on white drapes hung from the walls at the side, and music is provided by a professional sounding band – one of four that rotate week-by-week. Before the start of the service, a countdown clock encourages people to their seats five minutes before the band leader welcomes everyone and commences the service with a number of songs. The pastor speaks from behind a perspex lectern. Readings, lyrics and other congregational responses are projected onto two screens positioned either side of the stage. The congregation of 300 plus people is a wide mix of old and young – even to the extent that the church employs a dedicated children's minister to co-ordinate the volunteers that run the crèche and the other children's and youth groups. During the week, there are a number of smaller groups – mothers and toddlers, men's group, Bible study groups and an Alpha course – meeting in homes scattered around the town. This church is financially rich, full of willing people ready to volunteer for its various ministries and shows every sign of life and growth.

But here's the twist.

Many of the people who attend the growing warehouse church live within walking distance of the struggling local church and actually drive out to the industrial estate to attend the other. Some people even drive from neighbouring towns, to the detriment of their local churches. This church is the equivalent of the out-of-town supermarket. Why go to the trouble of shopping locally when you can get everything you want under one roof just a short drive away? And the excuses given for choosing the one church over the other are ultimately consumerist: 'This church doesn't meet my needs, so I will go somewhere that suits me better.' Or perhaps, 'The worship doesn't speak to me,' or even, 'This isn't my style of music, I prefer something a bit more lively.'

These peoples' choices regarding church are driven by notions of style and personal preference. The preaching style, the liturgical style and, perhaps most especially, the musical style. So market forces and *felt needs* decide which church survives and which dies out.

Let us continue to imagine, then, that, like any good business, the dying church looks to the successful church and says, 'What they're doing seems to work. Let's do what they are doing and we will be successful too,' and perhaps some generous soul leaves them a large bequest. What do they do with all that money? They look at the bigger, apparently successful, church on the industrial estate and buy a whole lot of new *stuff*. Maybe some blackout curtains to darken the church building and make their new coloured lights more effective, backing track software that makes it seem as if a full, modern band is leading their singing, a powerful new PA system that is probably too large for the type of building they have, and a perspex lectern for the preacher just like the one up the road, because that model of worship is successful *there*, so it must be successful *here*. 'The future of the church is digital,' they say, and hope that the slick new format will get people through the doors.

And here's twist number two: it works.

More people do indeed come through the doors. Some even start preferring the smaller chapel to the bigger warehouse because it is closer to home, or because it has a pleasant, more intimate, atmosphere. They like the style.

It's a bit more modern, a bit more relevant to 'where we're at.'[2]

But in the rush to bring everything up to date, to make it all *relevant*, nobody remembers to ask the question, 'Is it the right thing to do?' and as the church is now full, it must have been the right thing to do, surely. How can it be otherwise?

Quality vs. Quantity

The problem is, the assumptions that lie behind this scenario are all quantitative. Success is measured in terms of physical growth, rather than viewing the numerical as a by-product of spiritual quality. The new people that are filling the old church have just migrated from one place to another – this is not revival, these are not new Christians attracted by the spiritual life of mature disciples, merely church consumers who have found a brand that is more suited to their preferences.

As John Drane puts it in *The McDonaldization of the Church*:

> Being the church is not just about marketing, and a theology that comes pre-packaged, and in which there are no loose ends, is not true to life nor can it adequately reflect the richness of the gospel. Moreover, the key to efficiency in the business world is being able to process as many people as easily as possible. But Christian faith is not about processing people as if they were all peas in a pod.[3]

When we reduce church to a numbers game, importing the values of the business world into our faith, we say something fundamental about our thinking regarding the

---

[2] Drane, *McDonaldization*, 44.
[3] Ibid., 37.

nature of church. No longer do we suggest that faith embodies quality of community or relationship, either with each other or with God. A church focused on programmatic forms of corporate worship, demonstrated through the adoption of technological solutions to the issues of survival and growth, suggests that church is about little more than economics and financial viability, providing a product to individual consumers. This then has a profound impact on our ability to bring the gospel to non-believers, for 'if the church offers only the same things as the rationalized world of work, why should people who are oppressed elsewhere in their lives expect to find a resolution by joining the church?'[4]

As a consequence, we end up with a church ill-equipped to spread the gospel, unable to discuss complex theological concepts and with a limited understanding of what constitutes worship. Without quality and variety, the church as a whole struggles to reach out to any section of the population that does not listen exclusively to CCM[5] or understand the Christian faith as anything more than pseudo-psychotherapeutic *spirituality*. In the rush to relevance it is all too easy, instead, to become more disconnected from ordinary life and to retreat into a Christian sub-cultural bubble exacerbated by various Christian media – starting the day watching Christian TV, reading a Christian newspaper, travelling to work in the car listening to Christian radio and playing Christian music on an iPod at the gym, before coming home to eat with a Christian family and going out for the evening to church home group. There is no need for the coarseness and vulgarity of the secular world to impinge on life at all. No need to risk exposure to music that might have an ungodly

---

[4] Drane, *McDonaldization, 31.*
[5] Contemporary Christian Music.

influence, no need to talk with non-Christians if it can be helped.

This speaks of a faith bound by fear: fear that any contact with the so-called *real world* might somehow stop us from growing as Christians, fear that if we engage with the world around us that nice, glowing feeling we got from church or the latest conference might disappear and force us to deal with reality head-on. It seems to be that the churches that are the most successful numerically are the ones that cultivate those fuzzy feelings and do not challenge and provoke us into action.

> The practice of Christian worship in an age dominated by technology and technological thinking is in grave danger: in danger of becoming irrelevant and banal, in danger of becoming just another "technological fix", in danger of succumbing to the destructive values of technology, in danger of being locked into a religious or cultural ghetto, and yes, in danger of disappearing altogether.[6]

Churches that resort to programmatic, technological, *quick-fix* solutions can easily find themselves hindered in their ability to carry out contextual mission, growing stunted and immature disciples and, in the longer term, becoming stagnant, leading to a potentially terminal decline. The very problem which technology sought to solve leads to the church's downfall, simply because its priority lies in quantity rather than in quality.

Our use of technology within a corporate worship context can be uncritical and, consequently, damaging to the formation of healthy, mature disciples and to a vibrant, growing church. Which leaves us with a number of fundamental questions: firstly, given that we all live in a technological society, how should we relate to technology

---

[6] White, *Worship*, 128.

within our corporate worship environment? Secondly, if technology is uncreative and stunting, what does creative and vital corporate worship look like? Lastly, should we, as churches, embrace or reject the technological and what are the implications of each position in terms of our mission and the overall strength and health of the church?

What if, in a digital world, the future of the church is analogue?

1

WHAT IS TECHNOLOGY?

Technology is a word that describes something that doesn't work yet
— Douglas Adams

Douglas Adams once wrote that there are three kinds of technology, first, everything that's already in the world when you're born that's just normal; second, anything that gets invented between then and before you turn thirty which is incredibly exciting and creative and with any luck you can make a career out of it; and finally, third, anything that gets invented after you're thirty which is against the natural order of things and the beginning of the end of civilization as we know it until it's been around for about ten years when it gradually turns out to be alright really.[7]

Adams is correct, of course. Human beings became technological with the invention of the wheel, or perhaps with the discovery of fire, or at any point in history where we began to use tools to accomplish things. And consider how, in this computerized world, the technical support specialists for parents are very often their own children

---

[7] Adams, 'Worrying'.

and grandchildren. For the generations born since the 1980s or '90s, there has been no experience of life without TV, without computers, games consoles or Facebook. All this *stuff* is normal to them and there has always been a fear of change before the new norms become accepted - what Richard Hughes, in relation to contemporary art, called 'the shock of the new.'[8] So we must be careful that, however old or young we are, when we discuss technology, and particularly its role within corporate worship, that we do not fall into the trap of simply dismissing something because it falls outside our experience.

Similarly, in the field of music we must also take care as to how we define technology. Is the introduction of polyphony a technological advance? What about the invention of a new instrument like the organ, or the development of an existing one, such as the creation of the guitar from the viol, or changes to the nature of the orchestra? Can the very development of written systems of notation or of equal temperament be considered technological? Even some technologies unconnected to music caused changes to music itself. How did developments in architecture and the science of acoustics, for example, change the way music was composed and performed? Monteverdi, to take one example, wrote his *Vespers* in such a way as to take advantage of the specific acoustic characteristics of the Basilica of St. Mark's in Venice.[9] It is immediately clear, then, that technology of one sort or another has had a huge impact on the composition, performance and reception of music, and we need to investigate the nature and scope of this in order to generate an informed conclusion.

---

[8] Hughes, *New.*
[9] Wilson-Dickson, *Music,* 140.

Finally, we come to the church itself, where we must address issues of music and music technology since they so dominate our congregational expression that, for most, the very term *worship* has become almost synonymous with them. We must also consider the wider implications of technology on the way we conduct our services, on our musical choices, on the way we approach Scripture, on the depth of our theology and on our relationships within the congregation.

The Medium is the Message

Marshall McLuhan talks of the medium being the message; that even something as simple and ubiquitous as the electric light 'shapes and controls the scale and form of human association and action.'[10] He posits that, far from being simply a medium without any message (unless it is used as a neon advertising sign) that because artificial light is employed in human activity, be it baseball or brain surgery, it actually influences the nature and scope of those activities. So 'electric light and power... eliminate time and space factors in human association as do radio, telegraph, and TV.'[11]

McLuhan's argument is that technology of all sorts adds itself to what we already are; that devices become extensions of human nature.[12] So the railway, as he suggests, enlarges humanity's capacity for movement and changes society and the nature of our relationships as a consequence. For McLuhan, the gun is no longer a neutral tool that can be used for good or ill, but a technology that 'adds itself on to what we already are.'[13] So it is not simply used for good by good people and bad by bad people, but

---

[10] McLuhan, *Understanding*, 9.
[11] Ibid.
[12] Ibid., 12.
[13] Ibid.

carries with it a capacity to encourage aspects of our inherent nature.

As extensions and amplifiers of our very being, then, we must have great concern for how we employ technology within our corporate worship. The tools that we use to express our devotion to God have a profound effect on the nature of that devotion. And some, indeed, may well be incompatible with that devotion owing to the manner in which we behave as a result of their use. If certain technologies amplify the individual over the communal, the isolated over the relational, then are these technologies that we should encourage within our corporate worship expression?

All of these questions point us towards a definition of technology much wider than the world of electronic devices.

Definitions of Technology

Technology is everywhere. Even in make-up. You can buy LashFusion XL™ Micro-Technology Instant Lash Volumizer: 'A nutrient-rich volumizing mascara with patented Capisphere encapsulation technology'[14] which 'thickens, strengthens, conditions each and every lash, even after washing!'[15]

However nonsensical, advertisers know that to invoke the wonder of *technology* is to convey a sense of excitement, of cutting-edge science, of people in white coats slaving day and night to ensure that you, the consumer, have the very best mascara money can buy. *Technology* exists to make

---

[14] http://fusionbeauty.com/
[15] Only $24.00!

everyday life easier, people more beautiful and the world a better place. *Technology* is your friend.

Even as far back as the 1930s, scholars have endeavoured to provide an adequate definition as to what actually constitutes technology. American sociologist Read Bain came up with the following in 1937:

> Broadly conceived, technology is the most important single factor in producing, integrating and destroying cultural phenomena. Technology includes all tools, machines, utensils, weapons, instruments, housing, clothing, communicating and transporting devices and the skills by which we produce and use them. Social institutions, and their so-called non-material concomitants such as values, morals, manners, wishes, hopes, fears and attitudes are directly and indirectly dependent upon technology and are mediated by it.[16]

This is an extremely wide definition that has great strengths in its focus on the devices that we make and employ as well as the recognition that technology affects our worldview - our values, morals, manners and attitudes, as he puts it.

This is by no means a new idea. We can see it in action far back in antiquity. In Plato's *Phaedrus*, Socrates relates the oft-quoted story of *Thamus and Theuth*. In it, the god Theuth comes to Egypt to show to the Pharaoh Thamus the wondrous inventions he has made, 'desiring that the other Egyptians might have the benefit of them.'[17] Among the wonders he demonstrates for the king are arithmetic, geometry and astronomy - but his greatest discovery is that of writing. 'This,' says Theuth, 'will make the Egyptians

---

16 Bain, R., 'Technology', 860.
17 Plato, *Phaedrus*, Kindle ed., location 1394-1404.

wiser and give them better memories.'[18] But Thamus disagrees,

> This discovery of yours will create forgetfulness in the learners' souls because they will not use their memories; they will trust to the external written characters and not remember of themselves. The specific which you have discovered is an aid not to memory but to reminiscence, and you give your disciples not truth but only the semblance of truth; they will be hearers of many things and will have learned nothing; they will appear to be omniscient and will generally know nothing; they will be tiresome company, having the show of wisdom without the reality.[19]

Yet, in the twenty-first century we seem to have lost sight of this fact. *Technology* has become so ubiquitous, so interlaced with our every day existence, that we no longer consider the impact that it is having on the way we live - our attitudes, outlook and relationships. However, we must also take care that our definition of technology does not begin and end with consumer electronics. If it does, it is too easy to reduce the argument to a list of gadgets that are either a) Good or b) Bad. This is a trap of elephantine proportions that can reduce even the most civil of groups to a seething, bad-tempered debate as to the rights and wrongs of using the mobile phone at the breakfast table.

Radical French sociologist Jacques Ellul, writing in the 1960s, was keen to broaden the argument beyond devices and even beyond the standardization of the means of production. His concern was for the tendency towards efficiency and a 'single best way' of doing things that resulted from the increasing mechanization of society.

---

[18] Plato, *Phaedrus*, Kindle ed., location 1394-1404.
[19] Ibid.

The term *technique…* does not mean machine, technology, or this or that procedure for attaining an end. In our technological society, *technique* is the *totality of methods rationally arrived at and having absolute efficiency* (for a given stage of development) in *every* field of human activity [italics in text].[20]

Examining the Effects

Logically, then, we can examine technology as a whole – not by trying to argue that certain artefacts and procedures are technological while others are not, but by examining effects, in the same way that we can define *wind* by seeing the trees sway. In other words, we can define a system or device as *technology* or *technological* if it tends towards efficiency, uniformity or economy rather than valuing quality of life, uniqueness and creativity, or social justice. This is similar to what Stephen Monsma terms 'responsible technology' which seeks to define technology in the context of our relationships both to each other as beings created in the image of God, and to God himself.[21] He talks of the 'value-ladenness' of technology, which echoes McLuhan,

> Any technological object…embodies decisions to develop one kind of knowledge and not another, to use certain resources and not others, to use energy in a certain form and quantity. There is no purely neutral or technical justification for all these decisions. Instead they involve conceptions of the world that are related to such issues as permissible uses, good stewardship, and justice: they involve, in other words, human valuing.[22]

This leaves us with four overlapping categories into which we can place any given technology. On one axis we have

---

[20] Ellul, *Society*, xxv.
[21] Monsma, *Responsible*, 23.
[22] Ibid., 32.

hard or *soft* technology, which are the devices or systems that we use. This is epitomized in the computer which is both technological as a physical object (the hardware) and as the operating systems and other programs that it employs (the software). On the other axis we have *technology* versus *responsible technology* which can be determined both by the tendency towards the amplification or augmentation of a particular value-set, or by the manner in which we employ it. Admittedly this creates a somewhat complex relationship between ourselves and the devices and systems that we use, but at the same time it encourages a certain thought process by which we can evaluate their place within our Christian lives and corporate worship.

We must be careful, as well, not to consider *responsible technology* purely in relation to its use - that if, as Christians, we use a particular device or system in a way that assists the church in the fulfilment of the Great Commission, then it is automatically validated. *Responsible technology* acknowledges that 'the medium is the message,'[23] that it carries with it certain baggage in terms of what aspects of human nature it accentuates and augments, that technology is not simply our friend, but contains negatives as well as positives. It changes us, our relationships, our churches and even our whole society. We must learn to see that technology has an agenda all of its own, as Neil Postman says,

> Technological change is neither additive nor subtractive. It is ecological... One significant change generates total change... A new technology does not add or subtract something. It changes everything. In the year 1500, fifty years after the printing press was invented, we did not

---

[23] McLuhan, *Understanding*, 7.

have old Europe plus the printing press. We had a different Europe. [24]

So there are certain characteristics and tendencies that all technologies exhibit which must be considered in order to arrive at a properly balanced assessment of their impact upon the community - both Christian and non-Christian. The first of these characteristics is the manner in which it affects our attitude to time.

Time & Efficiency

In Europe, the first clocks were used in order to regulate the monastic life. According to Ellul, the first privately owned timepieces appeared in the sixteenth century and from then on, time has been divided into ever smaller increments. His argument maintains that in becoming subject to the precision of a mechanical device, mankind has become divorced from the rhythms and patterns of nature:

> ...since life is inseparable from time, life too was forced to submit to the new guiding principle. From then on, life itself was measured by the machine; its organic functions obeyed the mechanical. Eating, working and sleeping were at the beck and call of machinery.[25]

However subconsciously, and however dependent we are on the clock to regulate our lives, we struggle with the imposition of an artificial system upon the rhythm of our existence and create concepts such as the *work/life balance* in an attempt to gain control of the system. But we have created something over which we no longer have any control. For evidence of this, one only needs to witness the anger and frustration that bubbles up when a train is

---

[24] Postman, *Technopoly*, 18.
[25] Ellul, *Society*, 329.

five minutes late, or when a sermon over-runs. Our worldview, our universe, has become subject to an object that has no connection to the way in which our lives are meant to be lived:

> The machine tends not only to create a new human environment, but also to modify man's very essence. The milieu in which he lives is no longer his. He must adapt himself, as though the world were new, to a universe for which he was not created. He was made to go six kilometres an hour, and he goes a thousand. He was made to eat when he was hungry and go to bed when he was sleepy; instead he obeys a clock. He was made to have contact with living things, and he lives in a world of stone. He was created with a certain essential unity, and he is fragmented by all the forces of the modern world.[26]

So we fall back on survival strategies, we divide our lives and consequently our personalities into *free time* and *work time*, Ellul's 'essential unity' is fragmented by our need to cope with the demands that the clock imposes upon us. In *work time* we behave in one way, relate to our colleagues in a particular fashion, while in *free time* we behave and relate to people, possibly even the same people, in a different way. This is despite the fact that the concepts of *free time* and *work time* are largely illusory, simply ways of expressing different modes of *doing* rather than a manner of *being*.[27]

As our lives are compartmentalized, they become ever more quantifiable. Employers measure efficiency and effectiveness in the workplace by the quantity of work produced, and in a service economy where there is no physical outcome in production, by the amount of time spent at the desk. This is how working ever longer hours becomes a status symbol and a means of advancement

---

[26] Ellul, *Society*, 325.
[27] Greenfield, *People*, 104.

when the mechanisms already exist for us to actually work less. As Greenfield says, 'Being busy carries high status…The faster that new emails push those of a few minutes earlier up and off the screen, the more your cell phone sings out its tinny call sign, the more important you must be.'[28]

Back in 1932, Bertrand Russell's essay *In Praise of Idleness*, suggested that the working day should be a mere four hours long. He considered that we place more merit in production and work than we do in consumption and that in spending less time at work, people would have more energy and be more inclined to spend it in 'active pleasures', in our self-betterment, rather than in passive pastimes that result from exhaustion due to overwork.[29] Even as recently as July 2014, billionaire Carlos Slim suggested the introduction of the three-day working week.[30] It seems, however, that while some business leaders suggest it is viable, to make this switch would have a catastrophic effect on the global economy. For better or worse, our technology has locked us in to a particular pattern of work.

Speed, efficiency and economy seem to be the watchwords for the world of devices and these watchwords take no account of humanity. The clock creates the assembly line, and changes our view of the universe to that of a mechanical system. Ellul cites a study from the 1980s, by the Confederation Francaise et Démocratique du Travail, stating

> …insomnia is the basic problem of modern workers, and epidemiological studies show that heart and nervous problems have now spread to the working class. Yet we

---

[28] Greenfield, *People*, 102.
[29] Russell, 'Idleness'.
[30] Inman & Monaghan, 'Carlos Slim.'

have to point out that nervous fatigue is not solely due to the change in work. It is due to the modern lifestyle in general, the constant need to do everything faster, increasing life rhythms (fast food!), the multiplying of superficial human contacts, the tension of more and more crowded timetables. It is exhausting to live in a world in which everything is timed to the minute, in which there is never any time for rest... [31]

More recently, a study published in 2012 showed that 95% of people surveyed said 'they use their cell phone or computer within an hour of going to bed and as a result were experiencing poor sleep.'[32] It was also found that the artificial light from computer and cell phone screens 'suppress the sleep promoting hormone melatonin which supports the body's ability to sleep.'[33]

Increasingly, just as our ancestors worked to the speed of their production line machines, so we now work to the speed of our digital age and as a consequence our very physiology and psychology is being changed. Ellul is scornful of the speed of the modern world:

Time saved is empty time, I am not denying that on rare occasions speed might be of use, for example, to save an injured person, or to rejoin a loved one, or to go back to one's family, or for the sake of peace in a decisive meeting. But how few are the times when it is really necessary to save time? The truth is that going fast has become a value on its own... But experience shows the more time we save, the less we have. The faster we go, the more harassed we are... Without [the telephone, the telex, the plane] we would be no more harried that it was a century ago when we could all walk at the same pace.

---

[31] Ellul, *Bluff*, 43.
[32] Connelly, 'Switched-on'.
[33] Ibid.

> "You are denying progress then?" Not at all; what I am denying is that *this* is progress![34]

The speed of life makes us tend towards a reactionary stance rather than one of considered response. In fact, BBC Radio 4's *Today Programme* coined a word to describe the act of commenting on a speech that had yet to be given as a 'preaction'.[35] There is no room in the world any more for stillness and a considered response to a question. Debate devolves into argument and abuse more readily since there is no pause before response. To see this in action, one only needs to state something mildly controversial on social media. People react to their own prejudices rather than respond in thoughtful fashion, taking account of a point of view other than their own. 'Things are moving too fast to leave time for decisions.'[36]

Ellul considers that what we perceive to be progress is actually nothing of the sort - that our devices and systems are merely reiterations of what has gone before. We go fast because we can, rather than because we ought, and we sacrifice something of our humanity in doing so. This outlook on life, dating back as far as the 19th century, is seen by Postman as the birth of our consumerist society:

> ...we had learned *how* to invent things, and the question of *why* we invent things receded in importance. The idea that if something could be done it should be done was born in the nineteenth century. And along with it, there developed a profound belief in all the principles through which invention succeeds: objectivity, efficiency, expertise, standardisation, measurement, and progress. It also came to be believed that the engine of technological progress worked most efficiently when people are

---

[34] Ellul, *Bluff*, 258.
[35] BBC Radio 4, *Today*, broadcast 07/02/2014.
[36] Ellul, *Bluff*, 274.

conceived of not as children of God or even as citizens but as consumers - that is to say, as markets.[37]

This idea that all our problems can be addressed by a technological solution runs strictly counter to a biblical view of creation. Postman calls a society which invests technology with absolute, unquestioned authority and autonomy a 'Technopoly.'

> In Technopoly all experts are invested with the charisma of priestliness. Some of our priests are called psychiatrists, some psychologists, some sociologists, some statisticians. The god they serve does not speak of righteousness or goodness or mercy or grace. Their god speaks of efficiency, precision, objectivity. And that is why such concepts as sin and evil disappear in Technopoly. They come from a moral universe that is irrelevant to the theology of expertise.[38]

It is not for nothing that American sociologist Lewis Mumford called the clock 'the key machine' of the modern age.[39]

Homogenization & Standardization

Technology also has a strong, characteristic tendency towards standardization - to uniformity and repeatability. This is inherent in the nature of all things mechanical. The aim of any mechanism - physical or systemic - is to duplicate within a certain set of conditions. One obvious outcome of this is the ultimate destruction of spontaneity and creativity. Baroness Greenfield, however, considers that growing cultural homogenization may well be a small price to pay for a 'healthier and more fulfilled populace.'

---

[37] Postman, *Technopoly*, 42.
[38] Ibid., 90.
[39] Mumford, *Technics*, 14.

She qualifies it with the proviso – 'so long as the individual really is more fulfilled.'[40]

Once again, we must consider that this is a stance that considers only what we may gain from technological advance rather than looking at what we stand to lose. With a lack of cultural diversity and exposure to difference, there will be a lower tolerance of eccentric and unusual ideas. Consequently, it will become harder to express anything out of the ordinary, which is at the root of true creativity. Instead, we will be reduced to reinterpreting existing ideas rather than coming up with anything truly new. We will become subject to *McDonaldization*, sociologist George Ritzer's theory that claims that society is always given to seek the most efficient way of achieving a particular end, leading to what he terms 'formal rationality' - rules, regulations and bureaucratic systems that ensure a consistent outcome.[41] From package holidays to ready-meals to popular music, everything is manufactured to provide a uniformity of production and outcome so that the consumer knows exactly what he or she is going to get before they buy it.

So Greenfield's proviso regarding the fulfilment of the human being becomes moot. With systems, procedures and products that do not require the use of our special skills or abilities, the creative instinct within humanity will atrophy like an unused muscle. As Richard Münch puts it, 'We are captured by the iron cage of a McDonaldized world and are cut off from any ties to the authentic world in which we would be able to take part in producing and reproducing a life that we would consider a good one.'[42]

---

[40] Greenfield, *People*, 97.
[41] Ritzer, *McDonaldization*, 30.
[42] Münch, 'McDonaldized', 139.

In losing the elements of uncertainty and unpredictability, we become more risk-averse as a society, and less inclined toward experimentation and innovation in all sorts of fields. An open letter to *The Guardian*, in March 2014, from a number of senior academics suggested that even in the sciences, the structures surrounding research today are potentially hindering advance as there is no longer any space for the creative, maverick thinker.[43] Consider, too, from an artistic perspective, when the last time popular music truly tried to do something new, to push the boundaries in a spirit of true creativity, rather than merely reinterpreting existing forms, sticking to a tried and trusted formula known to be commercially successful.

At the root of the technological worldview is the manner by which everything becomes subsumed to its commercial potential. Even an art-form like music is reduced to nothing except its monetary value. The value of a painting is assessed in the auction house rather than in its historical or artistic significance. 'How much is it worth?' is the question that drives us, rather than the question of what it contributes to our culture and understanding of ourselves as creative or spiritual beings. As John Drane puts it, 'we have come to value one another mostly in mechanistic terms related to production and output.'[44] Or as the aphorism has it, we know the cost of everything and the value of nothing.

Jacques Ellul quotes essayist Antoine Mas who says,

> Standardization means resolving in *advance* all the problems that might possibly impede the functioning of an organisation. It is not a matter of leaving it to inspiration, ingenuity, nor even intelligence to find a solution at the moment some difficulty arises; it is rather

---

[43] Braben et al., 'Mavericks.'

[44] Drane, *McDonaldization*, 20.

in some way to anticipate both the difficulty and its resolution. From then on, standardization creates *impersonality*, in the sense that organization relies more on methods and instructions than on individuals [italics in text].[45]

Uniformity and repeatability values quantity over quality. And yet, counter-intuitively, in the midst of this abundance, we have less variety and less choice. This ties in with the notion of absolute efficiency associated with technology - or *technique* as Ellul calls the concept - the idea that there is 'one best way' of doing things.

Our lives become categorized and quantified by bureaucracy - intelligence tests, personality tests, educational institutions and the government all seek to tell us who we are and the one place we fit within the world for optimum economic efficiency in order to make money to support ourselves and our families. We define ourselves by what we do for a living.[46] Our educational systems, with their increasing focus on literacy, maths and science, seem targeted towards little more than to fit us for work, for economic productivity.

> The [technical] expert relies on our believing in the reality of technical machinery, which means we reify the answers generated by the machinery. We come to believe that our score *is* our intelligence, or our capacity for creativity or love or pain. We come to believe that the results of opinion polls *are* what people believe, as if our beliefs can be encapsulated in such sentences as "I approve" or "I disapprove."[47]

---

[45] Mas, as quoted in Ellul, *Society,* 11.
[46] The next time you are at a party try introducing yourself without mentioning work.
[47] Postman, *Technopoly*, 89.

Even our so-called rest and entertainment becomes nothing more than an opportunity to prepare for further work:

> ...the art of the culture industry... is the universality of the homogenous same, an art which no longer even promises happiness but only provides easy amusement as relief from labour: "Amusement under late capitalism is the prolongation of work. It is sought as an escape from the mechanised work process, and to recruit strength in order to be able to cope with it again."[48]

So in a fast food world we often choose to treat sustenance as 'fuel' rather than as an opportunity for fellowship and conversation.[49] There may be occasions where to treat a meal in this fashion might be convenient - we might be in a hurry, or grabbing a bite on a long journey, but to do so without awareness is to create a subtle shift in our thinking that legitimizes it each time we do it until we treat it as normal. Before too long we cannot conceive of the world in any other way. We must consider that if we continually disregard quality in favour of quantity then the former will suffer accordingly.

A further demonstration of the dangers of technological homogenization lies in the loss of linguistic diversity. As business is increasingly dominated by the digital, international market, English is rapidly becoming a global business language with a knock-on effect on everyday life. A study published in 2014 by Meta-Net details 21 languages that are at risk of 'digital extinction.' These are

---

[48] Adorno, as quoted by J M Bernstein from his Introduction, *Culture*, 7.
[49] Which in itself is a mechanistic mindset. A human being is merely a machine that needs to be 'refuelled'. If we are to value truly humanity as created in the image of God then these are images that we need to resist.

languages that may cease to exist as a result of the use of English as the *lingua franca* of global communication.[50]

Should this trend continue, we risk finding ourselves in a monocultural world that ceases to value humanity as anything other than a means of production. We may well be doomed to become a series of contradictions: talking a single language, but unable to relate to each other, a society which trumpets the rights of the individual and promoting individualization, while at the same time repressing individuality and uniqueness of character.

Progress & Passivity

The problem is that we have unleashed a digital revolution upon the world and we are in the very midst of its consequences without really understanding the full extent of what those consequences might be. According to Brynjolfsson and McAfee, 'Technological progress – in particular, improvements in computer hardware, software and networks - has been so rapid and so surprising that many present-day organizations, institutions, policies and mindsets are not keeping up.'[51] They suggest that globalization is not an explanation for this progress but rather 'a consequence of technology's increased power and ubiquity.'[52] The new, digital world is leaving some people, who have skills that have now become worthless, behind. Is it any wonder that some of these people, who have become marginalized by employers also feel threatened by the encroachment of the digital world into the sacred space of the church?

Technology creates passivity. In the same way a person who may have, in the past, worked on an industrial

---

[50] Ananaidou et al., *Language*, 21.
[51] Brynjolfsson and McAfee, *Race*, 8.
[52] Ibid.

production line and found themselves made redundant by a machine that can carry out the same task, we find that our devices are designed to be 'labour-saving,' so that food, for example, becomes fuel to be heated and consumed as quickly as possible - all part of the dehumanizing aspects of machines - and discards the social aspects of a meal altogether.

Supposed 'social' networking websites take the effort out of communication and even, on Twitter, restricting that interaction to a mere 140 characters. Rather than going to the effort of writing letters, people 'stay in touch' via Facebook, which essentially means that most peoples' relationships via the network are reduced to vague platitudes and cliché. To an extent, social networking simply exposes the superficial nature of our personal relationships in real life. We discover that it takes time and effort to truly get to know someone, and very quickly we find that, beyond the working environment, we have very little in common with them anyway. The people that we really get to know, the people that really matter to us are the people we make an effort to visit and spend time with. Facebook has taken the notion of friendship and turned it into a commodity - people gauge their status and popularity by the quantity of 'friends' they have on social media, rather than the actual quality of the relationships. Social media 'friendship' is friendship that makes no demands on us, or requires no sacrifice from us, and it is utterly disposable - all we need to do is 'unfriend' them when we get bored. As Roger Scruton has pointed out,

> Life in the actual world is difficult and embarrassing. Most of all, it is difficult and embarrassing in our confrontation with other people, who, by their very existence make demands that we may be unwilling to meet. It requires a great force, a desire that fixes upon an individual, and sees that individual as unique and irreplaceable, if people are to make the sacrifices upon

which the community depends for its longevity. It is far easier to take refuge in surrogates, which neither embarrass us nor resist our cravings.[53]

Baroness Greenfield offers similar warnings: 'If virtual friends replace flesh-and-blood ones, we shall not need to learn social skills, nor think about the unwanted and unpredictable reactions of others. So within this collective consciousness there need be no interaction, no action or response but rather, should we choose it, a passivity in which we are shielded from any disagreement or disharmony.'[54]

She considers, too, the psychological effects of our non-human interactions, echoing Scruton.

In fact, we shall inevitably find these artificial interlocutors more predictable, reliable, efficient and tolerant of our temper outbursts, stupidity and egotism. Gradually we could become more petulant, impatient, less able to think through problems, both social and intellectual, and utterly self-obsessed. And the poorer we become at social interactions the more we will seek solace with our cyber friends.[55]

We see this in microcosm in the reactionary nature of social media and the way that reactionary nature has transferred itself into our real life relationships and interactions. Meanwhile, websites such as Spotify give us more of the same as algorithms calculate more of what we want and recommend it to us. Thus we never grow outside of our own personal preferences and IT simply ends up reinforcing our prejudices.

---

[53] Scruton, *Culture*, 63.
[54] Greenfield, *Tomorrow*, 43.
[55] Ibid., 78.

Scruton also suggests a similar trend in our over-exposure to television as the passivity of our viewing habits means that it becomes harder for us to engage our minds and creative instincts. He suggests that in this, we substitute imagination for fantasy. In fantasy, we merely reinforce our own desires and cravings, focussing entirely on our own needs. As such, it is a commodity to be bought, or a drug that feeds sentimentality. It presents things explicitly, stripping away wonder or mystery. True imagination, he says, 're-orders the world, and re-orders our feelings in response to it… Where imagination offers glimpses of the sacred, fantasy offers sacrilege and profanation.'[56]

According to Douglas Groothius, meanwhile, television is 'an unreality appliance that dominates our mentality.'[57] In the UK, the average viewer watches nearly four hours of television per day.[58] Yet, how many of us actually give thought to how the TV is affecting our worldview? Technology is not neutral, 'the medium is the message' as Marshall McLuhan puts it.[59] It influences our thought patterns and our outlook on life, even if there is no evidence to suggest that it causes psychotic episodes, as some of the more lurid headlines surrounding violence in video games have suggested. However, to suggest that 'the camera never lies' is wrong. The camera is always lying - the camera shows us what the directors and the actors want us to see, not what is actually there. Even in news broadcasts, so-called factual reporting is changed by editors and reporters into something that is dramatic, that makes a good story - which is the essence of a modern news programme. Everything has become subsumed to the mantra of 'entertainment', because viewing figures (another example of the notion of quantity over quality)

---

[56] Scruton, *Culture*, 60.

[57] Groothius, *Decay*, 281.

[58] www.bbc.co.uk, 'Viewers.' 2014 figures from Thinkbox.

[59] McLuhan, *Understanding*, 7.

mean the success or failure of a particular network. Consider the following from Walter Benjamin:

> The artistic performance of a stage actor [i.e. what he or she does artistically] is presented to the audience by the actor in person; of that there is no doubt. The artistic performance of the screen actor, on the other hand, is presented to the audience via a piece of equipment, a film camera. The latter has two consequences. The apparatus that mediates the performance of the screen actor to the audience is not obliged to respect the performance as an entity. Guided by its operator, the camera comments on the performance continuously. The outcome of that running commentary, which the editor then assembles from the material supplied, is the film as finally put together… The second consequence is that the screen actor, by not presenting his performance to the audience in person, is deprived of the possibility open to the stage actor of adapting that performance to the audience as the show goes on; the cinema audience is being asked to examine and report without any personal contact with the performer intruding. *The audience empathises with the performer only by empathising with the camera* [italics in text].[60]

This is not to say that other media do not carry inherent biases of their own. Newspapers are an obvious example of how a liberal or conservative agenda can be emphasized by particular publications. There are, however, significant differences with televisual media. The first of these is the speed with which it reaches us. There is no chance to reflect and digest a news report, for example, before we have moved on to the next thing. Limitations of programme time prevent in-depth analysis and thought that could give information to help us understand the issue at hand. Print media, on the other hand, affords a certain degree of detachment. Even with a recognized political bias, there is an opportunity to consider wider

---

[60] Benjamin, *Work*, 17-18.

implications, to engage with a story and think about it further, to seek out other viewpoints. Television presents us with a picture and tells us what to think about it - the 'running commentary' of which Benjamin speaks. It is important that viewers question, then, whether TV reflects the world as it is or whether, as a society, we conform to the image that TV presents.

The primary danger in TV is when we use it as background for other activity. Groothius suggests that 'the triumph of the televised image over the word contributes to the depthlessness of postmodern sensibilities. Reality becomes the image, whether or not that image corresponds to any objective state of affairs - and we are not challenged to engage in this analysis.'[61] This indicates that there is a solution to the 'depthlessness' of which Groothius speaks: namely that if we engage in analysis, if we are active rather than passive in our engagement with media, consciously assessing quality and the nature of the representation being shown to us, then we can, to an extent, neutralize the damage it can cause.

Novelty & Need

Progress splits the world into digital 'haves' and 'have-nots' with the experts of the digital world endowed with the authority of priesthood – they are the *technorati*. The people who have the greatest respect within society today are not the artists, the creatives, the thinkers or the philosophers, but the scientists, the mechanics, the technicians[62] - those who are able to navigate the magical world of ones and zeroes. It is inevitable that this is a generational split - those for whom all this is normal become endowed with a status and quality that they would not have otherwise.

---

[61] Groothius, *Decay*, 286.
[62] All of which are professions with quantifiable outcomes.

Consequently, in a reversal of less technological cultures, those who have gained wisdom and experience by right of years are marginalized and looked down on by the young. The children no longer seek out the wisdom and respect of their elders, but the elders seek the digital savvy of the young, and society becomes the poorer for it. As Brynjolfsson says,

> Technology has advanced rapidly, and the good news is that this has radically increased the economy's productive capacity. However, technological progress does not automatically benefit everyone in a society. In particular, incomes have become more uneven, as have employment opportunities. Recent technological advances have favoured some skill groups over others...[63]

Monsma goes further,

> More and more people may feel that the emphasis placed on technological knowledge squeezes out the need for, and the time to pursue, spiritual knowledge. If so, then it is emphatically not the case that the direction of modern science and technology increases knowledge, but rather that it increases some *kinds* of knowledge at the expense of others.[64]

Everything that is new is lauded and the old is discarded. There grows a constant demand for novelty that is fed by companies in the name of profit and the old is discarded without any thought for what is being lost, or even whether it needs to be lost. Computers grow ever more powerful, but is the range of their ability to perform certain functions actually increased except in speed and efficiency? The mobile telephone is updated on a regular basis, but the one function that seems to be secondary in these upgrades is the ability of the phone to make and

---

[63] Brynjolfsson and McAfee, *Race*, 51.
[64] Monsma, *Responsible*, 35.

receive calls. Like magpies, consumers are attracted to the new and shiny. Desire and covetousness have become a compulsion. Status and self-worth is tied to the latest gadget: How old-fashioned we must be if we do not own the latest thing! 'Modern consumers have become so used to both the quantity of these sorts of technological objects and the continual parade of new ones that they now have difficulty determining what their true needs are.'[65] We have become blind to the difference between *need* and *desire*.

Positives of Progress

This all seems to place technology and technological progress in a very dim light. Surely there must be positives to progress?

George Ritzer's theory of McDonaldization is based around the four headings of efficiency, calculability, predictability and control, which mirror our own categories of time, homogenization, progress and novelty. As such, we are able to assess the positive aspects of technology, particularly in relation to church life, through these categories.

Efficiency allows timetables and allows us to work effectively. It helps coordinate global business and creates value-for-money. In a cash-strapped church economy efficiency is vital if a church is to be financially viable. The opposites of efficiency are wastefulness, bad organization, ineffectiveness and unprofessionalism. It could be said that a church that is wasteful, badly organized, ineffective and unprofessional will not survive in the modern world. It will not have the capacity to look beyond its walls, it will not be able to marshal its resources to mission or outreach.

---

[65] Monsma, *Responsible*, 120.

People looking in from the outside may only see a church struggling to survive in the wider marketplace.

Yet, efficiency can turn church into a business, a slick organization that has all the hallmarks of a thriving and profitable concern, but is in grave danger of focussing on the business aspects and forgetting the people. A church that has found Ellul's 'one best way' of doing things is expert in creating programmes and initiatives but lacks flexibility to deal with issues outside their sphere of expertise. The same can be said for their Sunday services - they will have a single expression of corporate worship that fails to address the breadth of age, experience or ethnicity that may be present within the congregation.

Calculability allows measurement. It creates the ability for organizations to measure progress. Calculability allows a church to measure how many people attend its various meetings throughout the week, and its Sunday services. This enables them to chart cycles of growth or decline, to assess the effectiveness of what they are doing in the community. Calculability enables a church to target certain groups and to tailor its outreach and services accordingly by the examination of local demographics.

A church that over-calculates, though, considers numbers as the be-all and end-all of their success. There is no sense of discipleship or spiritual growth because it is impossible to measure spiritual growth using any mathematical formula. It cannot accept that a vibrant, spiritually alive, spiritually mature church can have a small congregation. The only success it accepts is numerical, and it will seek to grow in those terms even at the expense of other congregations.

Predictability means that in any given environment a person will know what to expect. In the world of fast food this is modelled by global businesses like McDonald's, who ensure that a customer can go into any of their establishments in any country in the world and receive the same food, the same atmosphere and the same level of service. Predictability provides a minimum standard, it provides a sense of familiarity, safety and security for the customer. In this sense, predictability can be a positive. Ritzer himself notes, 'Customers take great comfort in knowing that McDonald's offers no surprises.'[66]

In some senses, a predictable church is a safe environment. A non-churchgoer can be invited to a Sunday service without fear. It will have a set programme, timed and lacking uncomfortable surprises. The people participating will have specifically defined roles and will be well-trained. There will be no participation from 'undesirable elements' that might spoil the atmosphere or be disruptive. Taken to a logical conclusion, however, a church which stifles all sense of unpredictability must surely lead to uncreativity. Spontaneity becomes difficult, or even impossible, as people are locked into behaviours that leave no room for individual expression. It must also lead to passivity among members of the congregation owing to a lack of general participation which, if left unchecked, becomes boredom.

While predictability ensures a minimum standard, this leads to individuals who perform to that level and no further. The food at McDonald's is made in a production line fashion, with no room for flair or variable quality. Consequently, it is (arguably) edible but no more. A hyper-predictable church will perform to a minimum standard, may very well have a large number of different ministries, but must, when considered logically, struggle to grow physically and spiritually because of its inability to think creatively.

---

[66] Ritzer, *McDonaldization*, 14.

The final aspect of Ritzer's thesis is that of control. This is tied very tightly to the notion of predictability in that control eliminates the unpredictable. The people in charge of various ministries will be properly vetted and trained to behave in a particular fashion. Positively, this brings a sense of accountability, of oversight. People involved in music, prayer, house group leadership and other ministries have clear tasks, perhaps even have written job descriptions and a reporting hierarchy or a system of mentoring.

These things are not bad in themselves, and in a national church that has been beset by allegations of abuse and sexual misconduct, proper oversight must surely be essential. These kinds of controls ensure a level of professionalism and education among those in leadership positions although a church with this at its heart can very easily tip over into cult-like control. There is always a temptation, however slight, to use one's training and position to dominate and manipulate, always the danger of using the pulpit to push one's own agenda. Excessive control puts influence in the hands of a few people, creates cliques and can lead to destructive power struggles.

So while there are clear positive aspects to each of the elements of McDonaldization, there are also some very strong negatives that, if left unchecked, can lead to the stagnation or even destruction of the local church. Ritzer himself suggests that we take advantage of the advances made possible by McDonaldization but reject its indiscriminate spread:

> Unfettered by the constraints of McDonaldized systems, but using the technological advances made possible by them, people could have the potential to be far more thoughtful, skilful, creative and well-rounded than they are now. In short, if the world were less McDonaldized,

people would be able to live up to their human potential.[67]

Conclusion

Technology is much more than just the machine. A broader definition grows out of our relationship to devices and systems and the attitudes and behaviours that surround them. We could question whether the machine is the symptom or the cause of these behaviours and attitudes. The answer, however, is that the machine is both cause and symptom. The machine both embodies and perpetuates a particular worldview. It is in no way neutral, but an extension of our beliefs and ideology, and our systems, which embed this ideology in society and its interaction, are themselves a form of technology and an accommodation with the devices we use.

> Technique integrates the machine into society. It constructs the kind of world the machine needs and introduces order where the incoherent banging of machinery heaped up ruins. It clarifies, arranges and rationalises; it does in the domain of the abstract what the machine did in the domain of labor. It is efficient and brings efficiency to everything.[68]

Technology makes us go faster than we should, presses us into schedules and patterns of living that are essentially unnatural, it can stifle creativity and diversity, as well as driving our consumption through an increasing desire for novelty and innovation, while creating passive and uncritical consumers.

At the same time we must allow that the clock enables us to co-ordinate and co-operate. As Einstein once put it,

---

[67] Ritzer, *McDonaldization*, 16.
[68] Ellul, *Society*, 5.

'Time is what prevents everything from happening at once.'[69] It would be nonsensical in a modern age to live without precise time-keeping, at least not without an apocalyptic restructuring of the world as we know it. So we are stuck with the world the way it is - with to-the-nanosecond scheduling, with devices that make it easy to replicate the things that we desire and need for survival (food, shelter and clothing), and with the joyful endorphin rush of buying shiny new gadgets from the internet or the Apple store.

McLuhan says that, 'Physiologically, man *in the normal use of technology...* is perpetually modified by it and in turn finds ever new ways of modifying his technology [italics mine].'[70] In other words, there is nothing we can do in terms of being changed by the tools and systems we use. Use of any technology, either primitive or complex cannot help but change us and we change it according to our desires and needs. What it does mean is that, this being the case, we can and must be particularly aware, when it comes to complex technologies, of the inevitable change and weigh the consequences both for good and for ill. The technophile will rush towards a positive conclusion, the technophobe to the negative, but a techno-synthesist will accept the existence of both and seek to weigh benefit against cost and attempt to mitigate it by taking action that preserves the positives of what is past. 'A preacher who confines himself to considering how a medium can increase his audience will miss the significant question: In what sense do new media alter what is meant by religion, by church, even by God?'[71] In this technological age,

---

[69] Actually, various people have had this aphorism ascribed to them. But it sounds to me like the kind of thing Einstein would come up with. So apologies to John Maynard Keynes and John Archibald Wheeler among others.

[70] McLuhan, *Media*, 51.

[71] Postman, *Technopoly*, 19.

which seems to be more about possessions and less about people and relationships, having an awareness of the impact of technology upon our lives is a step closer to challenging its autonomy and reclaiming responsibility for our own lives and the lives of our fellow human beings, instead of expecting our systems and devices to fix everything for us.

2

TECHNOLOGY AND MUSIC

Because you have things like 'American Idol' and you've got radio stations that play music made entirely by computers, it's easy to forget there are bands with actual people playing actual instruments that rock.

– Dave Grohl

Having established a definition of technology that creates an awareness of the technological beyond that of the *hard* technology of devices into the *soft* technology of systems and procedures, we can now begin to ask what impact the technological world of these devices and systems has had on the arts in general and on music in particular. Once we have established the extent of this impact, we can then proceed to examine how the attitudes shaped by technology have found their way into our churches and what, if anything, we can do to mitigate their effects – or indeed whether it is desirable to do so.

Music & Technology

Technological invention has always been at the forefront of progress in music. The invention of the flying buttress in medieval times led to the building of soaring cathedral spaces which in turn led to the emergence of polyphony.[72] Guido d'Arezzo's system of notation led directly to the stave that musicians use today. 'Notation,' Griffiths proposes, 'opens a distinction between composers (who create music that will last) and performers (who recreate that music for the moment).'[73] As a further example, it is clear that the invention of the organ transformed sacred music forever.

In more recent times, the emergence of the three minute pop song owes much to the length of recording time available on an old 78rpm record. This in turn, meant that jazz musicians in the early twentieth century were less free to create long improvisational passages, which in turn created a compositional formula that was suitable for recording and with it a measure of predictability. In other words, musicians were writing for recording rather than for freestyle, live performance. According to Mark Katz, 'The length of recordings and the brevity of solos remained constant for the thirty-one years between the first jazz recording and the introduction of the long playing record in 1948… and it affected jazz performance and composition alike.'[74]

Reproduction

The first commercially available gramophone was created in 1901 by the Victor Talking Machine Company. It was marketed not as a means of listening to music but as a musical instrument itself, intended to replace the piano as the main means of domestic music making.[75] Just one year later, Enrico Caruso had become the world's first

---

[72] Wilson-Dickson, *History*, 75-76.
[73] Griffiths, *History*, 6.
[74] Katz, *Capturing*, 86.
[75] Ross, *Listen*, 57.

recording star. Within thirty years of Thomas Edison's initial invention, recorded music was an established commercial product and set to break out of public space and into people's homes. Consider that prior to the 1870s, the only place one could hear music would be in the presence of the performer. With the invention of the gramophone, performance became divorced from hearing and the triumvirate of composer, performer and listener underwent a radical shift.

John Philip Sousa testified before US Congress in 1906, saying,

> These talking machines are going to ruin the artistic development of music in this country. When I was a boy... in front of every house in the summer evenings you would find young people singing the songs of the day or the old songs. Today you hear these infernal machines going night and day. We will not have a vocal cord left.[76]

Sousa feared that recording technology would signal the death of music and musicians, 'The time is coming,' he said, 'when no-one will be ready to submit himself to the ennobling discipline of learning music... Everyone will have their ready made or ready pirated music in their cupboards.'[77]

Similar prophecies of doom have been rehearsed for every development in musical technology since then. The release of the first CDs in the 1980s were greeted with howls of protest from those who had been brought up listening to music on vinyl that the supposed warmth and depth of their records had been stripped of their soul and turned into a clinical string of ones and zeroes. Since then, larger

---

[76] Sousa, J., as cited by Ross, *Listen,* 55.
[77] Ibid.

questions as to who owns music have been raised through the establishment of music streaming websites such as Spotify and last.fm.

Ultimately, Sousa was proven only partially correct in his assessment. Music has, indeed, become ubiquitous - witness the teenager *sodcasting*[78] on the bus as a prime example - and it is true that everyone does have ready made music in their cupboards, so to speak. These days there is no escape from the sound of music. As Slouka says, 'Ensnared in webs of sound, those of us living in the industrialised West today must pick our way through a discordant, infinite-channeled auditory landscape... Everywhere a new song begins before the last one ends, as though to guard us against even the potential of silence.'[79] At the same time, though, people continue to take up musical instruments, inspired by their musical heroes and heroines, making it possible to argue that recording technology has, in fact, broadened our ability to explore musical forms as we gain access to the music of other cultures through the Internet.[80]

To consider recorded music simply as an extension of *live* performance, however, would be incorrect. Postman suggests of television, for example, that 'to make such a mistake... is to misconstrue entirely how television redefines the meaning of public discourse. *Television does not extend or amplify literate culture*. It attacks it... What is television? What kinds of conversations does it permit? What are the intellectual tendencies it encourages? What

---

[78] 'Sodcasting – verb. The act of playing music through the speaker on a mobile phone, usually on public transport. Commonly practiced by young people wearing polyester, branded sportswear with dubious musical taste.' http://www.urbandictionary.com

[79] Slouka, M., 'Listening,' 41.

[80] Broadened our ability, perhaps, but not necessarily in fact as we shall see later on.

sort of culture does it produce [italics mine]?'[81] In the same way, neither is recorded music simply an extension or amplification of its earlier form allowing us to apply the questions Postman asks of television to the phenomenon of recorded music. Does recorded music attack musical culture? What musical or emotional expression does it permit? What intellectual tendencies does it encourage? (or indeed, what tendencies does it atrophy?) What sort of culture does it produce?

Glenn Gould, renouncing live performance in 1964, predicted the disappearance of the concert hall within a century, but far from seeing this as a negative development, he saw it as overwhelmingly positive, as people were exposed to a wider musical world.[82] The question we must ask ourselves is whether *live* performance represents the pinnacle of musical perfection.

The main issue with recorded music must be its lack of context. 'Reproductive technology,' Benjamin states, '…removes the thing reproduced from the realm of tradition. In making many copies of the reproduction, it substitutes for its unique incidence a multiplicity of incidences. And in allowing the reproduction to come close to whatever situation the person apprehending it is in, it actualizes what is reproduced.'[83] It is clear, then, that a piece of music has a tradition and a context. In its technological reproduction, the piece is divorced from its initial context - the place of performance - and this must be so because time passes. Mechanical reproduction, however, bypasses context altogether as the place one can play a piece of music is determined only by the technology available to the individual. One can listen to a Mozart Requiem on the bus, or to Foo Fighters in one's bedroom.

---

[81] Postman, *Amusing*, 86.
[82] Ross, *Listen*, 56.
[83] Benjamin, *Work*, 7.

Is the piece of music as art invalidated once it is produced more than once? Is the artistic nature of music tied up with its ephemeral nature? Surely not! In live performance, each time music is re-performed, the original context is taken and reinterpreted and as each reinterpretation is made for new contexts and new generations, the weight of tradition and power of experience builds.

At the same time, for recorded music, the appreciation of a piece grows through knowledge of the context within which it was composed and performed. Take, for example, Leonard Bernstein's recording of Beethoven's ninth symphony, made on Christmas Day 1989.[84] A hugely well-known piece of music which has been recorded in many different versions by many different conductors and orchestras. Bernstein's recording, however, preserves a particular moment in time - namely, the celebrations surrounding the collapse of the Berlin wall and the reunification of Germany after 40 years of communism. The piece is shot through with the emotion of the momentous political events that surround it and it is only in knowing this context that one can fully appreciate the power of the music against its technical imperfections.

Through the passage of time, the listener becomes increasingly divorced from the live performance and its context, its true power only partially recaptured when one understands the circumstances of the performance. Music's value lies in more than its notes and sounds, but in the ritual and tradition that surrounds it. According to Katz, 'before the advent of recording, listening to music had always been a communal activity... Listening was a culturally significant activity... Solitary listening, then, contradicted centuries of tradition...'[85]

---

[84] http://www.naxos.com/
[85] Katz, *Capturing*, 20-1.

So Gould must be wrong in his assessment. If music is so psychologically bound up with community, people will always have reason to witness, will always find greater significance in the visceral nature of a live performance than in listening to a recording, or in watching on television. Music has a greater power in its immediacy and in its transient nature. The concert hall is here to stay, provided people are given the option. The danger is, of course, with so much widespread cheap, recorded music, and with the various costs and occasional sense of elitism associated with attending a concert, that people will have less and less motivation to experience a live performance.

The studio creates a new context for music, placing the concert hall under extreme pressure, bringing a fourth player into the relationship between composer, performer and listener: the engineer. Through increasing digitization, the context of the performer has become fictionalized. Musicians are recorded individually, while overdubbing and auto-tune give them a perfection that is unobtainable in real life. Meanwhile, reverb effects create a sonic illusion - a space which doesn't actually exist at all. The technology of recording strips the heart and soul of humanity from the *performance*. 'The virtual studio, then, is... the fictional setting where stories take place... a facsimile of a bloodless operating theatre, a chemist's laboratory lacking in smells or fire.'[86]

Consequently, a false impression and an unrealistic expectation is created in the mind of the listener, an illusion that is shattered by the live performance of the concert hall. 'The phenomenon of the "dummy star" who has a hard time duplicating in the concert hall what he or she purports to do on record, is not unheard of.'[87] This is a

---

[86] Toop, *Ocean*, 125.
[87] Ross, *Listen*, 61.

seeming reversal of the initial purpose of recording. Where in early years, recordings were made with the express purpose of preserving valuable or significant performances, now the live performance seeks to do nothing less than duplicate the recording. Ross says that, 'When they [musicians] went back onstage, they tried to embody the superior self that they had glimpsed in the phonographic mirror, and never again played in quite the same way.'[88]

Katz believes that 'For many listeners… music is now primarily a technologically mediated experience. Concerts must therefore live up to recordings…'[89] The listener expects the concert to match the expectations built up by the record while the performer is influenced by the precise demands of the studio. Any individual expressiveness through the use of vibrato, vocal or instrumental improvisation or from singing a note fractionally too short or too long, or any other such idiosyncrasies are all eliminated by the diktats of a digital age that prizes technical accuracy over emotional content. *Dead air* - long moments of silence - is considered something to be avoided, so performances are tightened to minimize these moments.[90] Likewise, the lack of an audience creates a struggle for performers to generate the emotional depth of the music which is often communicated in non-musical ways, through facial expression or body movement. All of these factors in the studio eventually spill over into the performance space as artists endeavour to reproduce their *superior* studio selves.[91]

Ross argues, however, that classical music stands somewhat outside this mediated realm, owing to the way

---

[88] Ross, *Listen*, 63.
[89] Katz, *Capturing*, 31.
[90] Ibid., 28.
[91] Ross, *Listen*, 63-64.

sound is produced. 'Most of its repertory is designed to resonate naturally within a room,' he says.

> By contrast, almost all pop music is written for microphones and speakers. In a totally mediated society, where some form of electronic sound saturates nearly every minute of our waking lives, the act of sitting down in a concert hall, joining the expectant silence in the moments before the music begins, and surrendering to the elemental properties of sound can have an almost spiritual dimension.[92]

This idea of the *organic* nature of certain music need not be restricted to the orchestra or the concert hall. There is similar power in acoustic folk, blues or country music. Deriving from a depth of tradition and context and performed acoustically, it can be as emotionally powerful as a symphony.[93] However, that semi-spiritual power is lost in the commercial demands of recorded, manufactured pop music.

This all feeds perfectly into Ritzer's McDonaldization categories. Recorded music must be efficient in order to fit onto finite media formats, it is calculable through its commodification and tracking of sales through the charts, it is ultimately predictable through its repeatability both in the mass production of recordings and as the recordings feed back into live performance, as we have seen. Finally, control comes through the homogenization of musical forms - music streaming websites increase the ability to hear radically different kinds of music, but their

---

[92] Ross, *Listen*, 66.

[93] Listen to a recording of Johnny Cash singing *San Quentin* live at San Quentin prison. The emotion and tension generated there still crackles through the recording. Even though it might be argued that Cash is not a particularly technically proficient singer or guitar player, it is not his technical skills that generate the power of the performance, rather it is the performance's content and context.

recommendations ensure that individuals are given more of what they already like. Far from encouraging exploration and experiment, they limit people's listening habits even further.

Commodification

Recording has created a world where music is no longer special, happening only when musician and listener occupy the same space. 'Music is everywhere'.[94] So much so that even as far back as 1969, the General Assembly of the International Music Council at UNESCO published the following resolution:

> We denounce unanimously the intolerable infringement of individual freedom and of the right of everyone to silence, because of the abusive use, in private and public places, of recorded or broadcast music. We ask the Executive Committee of the International Music Council to initiate a study from all angles - medical, scientific and juridical - without overlooking its artistic and educational aspects, and with a view to proposing to UNESCO, and to the proper authorities everywhere, measures calculated to put an end to this abuse.[95]

Where music had once been an ephemeral art form, only becoming substantive in its realization through performance, recorded sound - or what Katz terms 'mediated sound' - became a physical object.[96] And while the concert had, since the time of Purcell in the 17th century, been a paid-for experience,[97] it can be argued that the widespread distribution of the printed score, vinyl disc, cassette and CD increasingly turned music from an art into a product. As Katz says, 'When performed live, musical

---

[94] Griffiths, *History*, 230.
[95] as cited in Shaffer, 'Environment,' 37.
[96] Katz, *Capturing*, 2.
[97] Griffiths, *History*, 104.

sound is fleeting, evanescent. Recordings, however, capture these fugitive sounds, tangibly preserving them on physical media... Once musical sound is reified... it becomes transportable, saleable, collectable and manipulable in ways that had never before been possible.'[98]

It all started in the 1890s, as 'alert entrepreneurs' placed phonographs in penny arcades.[99] It grew to become a teenage rite of passage, going into the record shop to buy your first LP. If you were lucky, the store assistant would suggest other things you might like, or else cast a disdainful look at your choice in music. But as recording changed listening into consuming, performance into reproduction, and composition into sonic illusion, three developments of the 1980s completed the transformation of music into full-blown commodity. These were the home computer, which in turn gave rise to the home studio; the digital synthesizer, which created many a bedroom pop-star; and the advent of MTV, which shifted music away from sound towards image.

Analogue synthesizers had been used as far back as the 1950s in the experimental music of Pierre Schaeffer, Karlheinz Stockhausen, Milton Babbitt and Terry Riley. Robert Beyer's 1951 piece *Sound In Unlimited Space* is widely credited as the first piece of synthesized music.[100] By 1956 *Forbidden Planet*, the classic science-fiction reinterpretation of Shakespeare's *The Tempest* starring Leslie Nielsen and Robbie the Robot,[101] distinguished itself in cinema and musical history by having a soundtrack entirely composed

---

[98] Katz, *Capturing*, 4.
[99] Ross, *Listen*, 57.
[100] Ross, *Noise*, 429.
[101] Not necessarily in that order.

of electronic tones.[102] Subsequently, the Mixtur-Trautonium, a predecessor to the synthesizer invented in Berlin in the 1920s achieved its moment of glory as the source of the birdcalls used by Alfred Hitchcock in his 1963 adaptation of Daphne du Maurier's *The Birds*.

At the 1967 Monterey Pop Festival, Jimi Hendrix attempted to set fire to his guitar, The Who demolished their set and, more significantly for our purposes, the Moog Synthesizer was showcased for the very first time. It was readily adopted by rock-pop and classical musicians alike, but it wasn't until the 1980s, when the synthesizer became digitized, that it was liberated from the ivory towers of IRCAM[103] and the Columbia-Princetown Electronic Music Centre[104] and moved into the homes of ordinary people. With the creative possibilities expanded by connection to rapidly developing home computers and to other keyboards via MIDI[105] the home studio was born and with it, the rise of a new form of electronic pop music.

Sheffield Polytechnic[106] was the rather unlikely venue for the birth of electro-pop in the UK. Heaven 17, ABC and Human League were all performers there. Their avowed aim - to destroy rock music.[107] Philip Oakley freely admits that Human League picked up synthesizers because they were too lazy to learn guitar. Not everyone was happy about this new ethos. According to Simpson, 'Their [Human League's] nemesis was the Musicians Union, which saw synthesisers and drum machines as a threat to

---

[102] Now an acknowledged classic, this film was unrecognised by the American film industry at the time, receiving just a single Oscar nomination for its special effects.

[103] Institut de Recherche et Coordination Acoustique/Musique.

[104] Home of the first RCA MkII Electronic Music Synthesiser.

[105] Musical Instrument Digital Interface, released in 1983.

[106] Now Sheffield Hallam University.

[107] Simpson, 'Riot'.

the livelihood of thousands of percussionists.'[108] The union launched the 'Keep Music Live' campaign in response. Human League reacted by producing their own slogan: 'Keep Music Dead.'[109] "'We hated anything that wasn't modernist," says ABC's Martin Fry. "It was like Cavaliers and Roundheads. Total warfare!'"[110] Human League's chance came when Virgin Records gave them their big break off the back of the label's prior success with Mike Oldfield's *Tubular Bells*. A movement that took its lead from the experimentalism of Kraftwerk and Brian Eno crossed over into the mainstream. And it needed an image.

MTV was launched in 1981. It was the first 24-hour rolling music video channel and it coincided perfectly with the surge of New Wave artists like Depeche Mode, Gary Numan and Duran Duran. The ease with which electronic music could be produced was a gift to the record labels and coupled with the increasing image-consciousness fuelled by MTV, appearance rapidly took over from musical considerations. Now the good-looking yet talentless could find an audience. Nowhere is this more vividly illustrated than in the case of Milli Vanilli.

The album *Girl You Know It's True* was released in 1989, spawned three Number One hits and sold over seven million copies. To all intents and purposes, this was an immensely successful commercial venture. But there was one problem. Milli Vanilli - Fabrice Morvan and Rob Pilatus - did not sing a single one of their songs, instead lip synching to pre-recorded tracks by Johnny Davis, Charles Shaw and Brad Howell. The story broke in 1990 shortly after Milli Vanilli had just been awarded the Grammy for Best New Artist. The award was rescinded as a result of

[108] Simpson, 'Riot'.
[109] Ibid.
[110] Ibid.

the scandal and remains the only time this has ever happened.[111] At the time, producer Frank Farian turned down an offer from Morvan and Pilatus to sing, stating that, 'I don't go for that. Sure, they have a voice, but that's not really what I want to use on my records.'[112] Farian wanted to create an attractive product with Morvan and Pilatus' image, but without their voices. Speaking in 2010, Morvan noted, 'What we were crucified for, you see everywhere. Society and life and everything changes.'[113]

When Susan Boyle appeared on *Britain's Got Talent*[114] in 2009 for the first time, the audience expectation was of a disaster waiting to happen. According to the *Washington Post*, 'The eye-rolling public and the three jaded judges were waiting for her to squawk like a duck.'[115] This expectation was based entirely on her image. Her subsequent success was trumpeted as a triumph of musical talent over looks and the usual airbrushed, PR managed pop star cliché. Her success derived from the fact that she was 'everyman' (or woman in this case). She was the housewife made superstar, boosting ratings for the show and putting more money into the pockets of record producers precisely because of her apparent ordinariness, simply because it suddenly seemed that maybe the dreams of the shower-singing diva might actually be within grasp. Paradoxically, this image was, of course, carefully managed. Ultimately, however much it was supposed to be 'all about the music', it was actually still all about the image even though, in this case, it was a carefully marketed lack of pretension.

---

[111] Philips, 'Grammy'.
[112] Farian, quoted in Philips, 'True'.
[113] Morvan, quoted in Shriver, 'Scapegoats'.
[114] Another Simon Cowell production.
[115] McManus, 'Defiant'.

Theodor Adorno says that 'the hit song enthusiast must be reassured that his idols are not too elevated for him, just as the visitor to philharmonic concerts is confirmed in his status.'[116] but Adorno is not quite correct in his assessment. If an idol is placed within grasp then the sham is too easily spotted. If, conversely, an idol is too elevated then there is nothing to which the person-in-the-street may aspire. Produce an idol who appears ordinary, however, but remains just out of reach and viewers will always retain their dream of 'it could be me.' None of this has anything to do with musical ability and everything to do with product marketing. 'With MTV,' suggest the Weinsteins, 'pan-capitalism becomes hyper-capitalism. Originally an advertisement for a band, when the music video becomes the interpretative frame for rock music, it remains an advertisement... MTV is an ad that is incidentally meant to be consumed as an art-entertainment... it sells an audience to advertisers.'[117]

The music of computer, synthesizer and MTV is the product of an age where life is increasingly geared towards economic production. One is forced to agree with Adorno's statement that, 'Amusement under late capitalism is the prolongation of work. It is sought as an escape from the mechanised work process, and to recruit strength in order to be able to cope with it again.'[118]

Scruton extends the idea still further, to go so far as to deny that commodified music is music at all, 'The postmodern world denatures music only because it denatures everything, in order that each individual might have his chance to buy and sell. Popular music ceases to be music, just as sexual love ceases to be love...'[119]

---

[116] Adorno, 'Fetish,' 35.
[117] Weinstein & Weinstein, 'Enframed,' 68.
[118] Adorno, as cited by Bernstein, 'Introduction', 7.
[119] Scruton, *Aesthetics*, 505.

In this rather bleak assessment, we lose art and culture because they have become products to be bought and sold. Everything is reduced to utility and marketability, including our souls expressed through artistic form. This in turn, kills transcendent faith. 'Through melody, harmony and rhythm,' Scruton suggests, 'we enter a world where others exist besides the self, a world that is full of feeling but also ordered, disciplined but free. That is why music is a character-forming force, and the decline of musical taste a decline in morals.'[120] He is not, however, advocating musical snobbery. 'By scorning the common culture… it also scorns the social existence which makes culture of any kind possible. The aristocratic contempt for the market-place is a two-edged weapon which, wounding the community, wounds also itself. For it damages the common life upon which all individual gestures, however original, however sublime, depend for their significance.'[121] 'Common' culture has value, and we must be careful that in discussing issues of commodification we do not find ourselves rejecting music that has an artistic, cultural value simply because it has become commodified. Which leaves us with a fundamental question. How do we decide what is 'good' music?

Homogenization

Researchers from the Spanish National Research Council noted that across a fifty year timescale, up to 2010, transitions between chords, note combinations, tone and instrument choices all became less and less diverse over time, while the songs themselves grew increasingly louder. Tunes today, researcher Joan Serrà observed, restrict themselves to a 'fashionable' set of chords and a uniform high volume throughout.[122] It would appear that the idea

---

[120] Scruton, *Aesthetics*, 502.
[121] Ibid., 473.
[122] Wolchover, 'Music'.

of technology opening up new creative vistas and democratizing music-making is a myth. In reality, when we allow machines to make and mediate our music, we lose, rather than gain, creativity and imagination as technical perfection supersedes passion, tradition and context. A combination of commodification and increasing digitization blunts our creative instincts. Australian cultural anthropologist Genevieve Bell, speaking at TEDx, Sydney in 2011, suggests our constant access to mobile phone and internet curtails our ability to innovate – we consume but we fail to develop our own point of view. It becomes, in her opinion, easier to chase after existing ideas than to come up with new ones.[123] This is certainly true of popular music.

Even as the avant-garde movement, typified by the music of Schoenberg and Stravinsky, became less and less accessible, it still sought to define music in relation to an audience.[124] But pieces created by groups such as Fluxus and the Scratch Orchestra were soon rejected in favour of a new, listener-friendly tonalism, emerging in the minimalist music of composers such as Steve Reich, Terry Riley and Philip Glass. Meanwhile, Brian Eno, keyboard player for Roxy Music, blurred the boundaries between 'classical' and 'pop' in the creation of his albums *Music For Airports* and *Another Green World,* creating a new genre of 'ambient music'. The music of modern composers Arvo Pärt and Henryk Górecki seems to owe more to this tradition than to the extreme atonalism of Boulez or Gerard Grisey. Steve Reich has even produced a piece, *Radio Rewrite,* directly influenced by the music of Radiohead.[125] So-called 'serious' composers permitted themselves to be influenced by popular streams and vice versa.

---

[123] Bell, as quoted in Connelly, 'Switched-on'.
[124] Nyman, *Experimental,* 11.
[125] Petridis, 'Reich'.

All this in aid of music that appealed to the listener, rather than being centred on the performer, as happened with Cage and the experimental music movement.[126] It is said of Cage that, 'The tasks of experimental music do not generally depend on, and are not markedly changed by, any response from the audience, although the atmosphere in which these tasks are accomplished may be completely changed by audience response.'[127]

According to Reich, though, 'What my generation did wasn't a revolution, it was a restoration of harmony and rhythm in a whole new way, but it did bring back those essentials that people wanted, that people craved, but in a way they hadn't heard. Now we're living back in a normal situation where the window is open between the street and the concert hall.'[128]

But seeking to define music in relation to an audience means that it is too easy to shift from a serious exploration of musical form and its limitations, to creating a people-pleasing formula that can be replicated at will, heavily marketed and mass produced. As we have already seen, the technology available makes producing and reproducing these formulae immensely easy and, above all, cheap. With the phonograph effect placing limits on vocal and instrumental style, and eliminating almost all traces of individuality, songs become mere mechanical objects, devoid of thought and emotion. The vocalist need not even be especially talented when auto-tune can correct a multitude of sins.[129] All that matters is that production costs are kept low for the sake of maximum profit.

---

[126] Nyman, *Experimental*, 14.
[127] Ibid., 23.
[128] Reich, quoted in Petridis, 'Reich'.
[129] Adorno, 'Fetish,' 37.

> Today's instruments require no expertise in reading or writing music notation, and users need no prior experience with playing instruments. Samplers and synthesisers allow musicians to cull together instrumental sounds with a mouse, and editing software makes possible the importation of sound effects, acoustic spaces, and even apparatus sounds of old playback equipment.[130]

This has not gone unnoticed. In 2009, rap-metal group Rage Against The Machine launched a campaign to get their song *Killing in the Name* to number one in the UK charts in time for Christmas.[131] The following year, a group made up of artists, musicians and stand-up comics recorded a version of John Cage's *4' 33"* for their bid to become Christmas number one, dubbing themselves, in homage to the previous year, Cage Against The Machine.[132] Both of these campaigns were protests against the seemingly never-ending procession of manufactured pop acts emerging from Simon Cowell's *The X-Factor* programmes.[133] Instinctively, musicians and artists recognize that music made in a production line fashion is no music at all.

This mass-produced music is not even made to be listened to, but rather to be the soundtrack to everyday life – what Joanna Demers terms 'ambient listening.'[134] Ambient listeners tune in and out of music, and use it to provide a counterpoint to the monotony of the working day and the daily commute. It is nothing more than a mood modifier,

---

[130] Demers, *Listening*, 9.

[131] Jones, 'Cowell'.

[132] Ewing, 'Cowell'.

[133] *Rage Against the Machine* were successful in their protest, beating X Factor winner Joe McElderry to the top spot. *Cage Against the Machine*, meanwhile, could only manage number 21, beaten by X Factor's Matt Cardle.

[134] Demers, *Listening*, 16.

encouraging productivity on the shopfloor or in the office.[135] It plays constantly on the radio in the background, or on portable media players.[136] According to Demers, listening to electronic music is intermittent and interrupted; listeners may come and go at a venue, or press pause on their device to return to where they left it later on, or they may carry on a conversation at the bar while music plays in the background.[137] Her overall assessment of the phenomena is stark, '…electronic music forecasts the end of music as we have known it in the West for several centuries… Music as any form of organised sound will continue to exist… But the rituals and expectations surrounding this experience have changed and promise to continue to do so.'[138]

In Western popular music, we have become caught in a downward spiral perpetuated by the need to produce music that can be half-listened to, or at least that has a regular beat that can be danced to in a nightclub (for which the mathematical certitude of electronic music is ideally suited). With the growth of computing power and music technology, the disco music of the 1970s was quickly supplanted by the electronic dance music of the '80s and '90s simply because of the ease by which such music could be produced. As Demers says, 'Virtually anyone with a personal computer can afford to produce professional-quality electronic music from inside the home for less than a few hundred dollars. In short, digital

---

[135] Ball, *Instinct*, 271.

[136] Even the dedicated mp3 player has largely vanished in the last decade, replaced by the convergent technology of the mobile phone, many of which are not even advertised as phones at all but as devices through which we can access music, video, photographs and the Internet.

[137] Demers, *Listening*, 17.

[138] Ibid., 153.

synthesizers have made music making more egalitarian than at any other time in history.'[139]

This could be applauded - music making has become democratized. Now anyone can make professional sounding music from the comfort of their own home studio. 'When the Beatles wanted strings on their recordings, they had to bring in trained musicians. Whether employing a string quartet or an orchestra, the costs were prohibitive. Today, a single instrument contains hundreds of sounds - strings, orchestras, organic folk instruments - literally anything a musician needs. Technology begat musical democracy.'[140] But a great deal of the music produced in the bedroom is little more than a regular beat and an unsophisticated bass line. There is no melody, no harmony, not even an arrangement save that the bass line occasionally stops for a few beats and with the rise of the home studio, the isolation of individual musicians is complete, for now musicians need not ever meet to play together. The community aspects of music-making may well die out altogether, completing the journey begun by the rise of recorded music and the technological demands of the studio.

Scruton and Adorno agree that 'the musical experience… has become truncated, embryonic, reduced to an external pulse and often surrendered to the machine… where there is no melody to speak of, where the rhythm is machine made, and… the only invitation to dance is… with oneself.'[141] This is termed 'regressive listening,' as the coarsening of music hinders our ability to accept anything more refined. Adorno says, 'There is a neurotic mechanism of stupidity in listening… the arrogantly ignorant rejection of everything unfamiliar is its sure sign. Regressive listeners

---

[139] Demers, *Listening*, 9.
[140] Detweiler & Taylor, *Matrix*, 150.
[141] Scruton, 'Soul'.

behave like children. Again and again with stubborn malice, they demand the one dish they have once been served.'[142]

Sentimentality

Music's affective power lies, to a certain extent, in its unpredictability - what Meyer and Ball term 'deviation.'[143] As certain experiences within culture produce certain expected, almost Pavlovian responses, the affective power of music declines in line with its predictability. 'The customary or expected progression of sounds can be considered as a norm which, from a stylistic point of view, it is; and alteration in that expected progression can be considered a deviation. Hence deviations can be regarded as emotional or affective stimuli.'[144]

Physiological stimuli, though, do not constitute the whole story.[145] Certain chord sequences, melodic and harmonic motifs can create a sense of emotion, but this is a long way from saying that this creates *good* music. Emotiveness is by no means a measure of quality. It is, as we have already seen in contrast with Bernstein's Beethoven, possible to be technically perfect but emotionally barren. Conversely, it is also possible to have what Ball terms 'low' music that is emotionally rich.[146] Neither is the atonal and unpredictable music of the experimental movement affective since there is no structure to which people can align their experience. 'Affective experience is just as dependent on intelligent cognition as conscious intellection... both involve perception... [So] thinking and feeling need not be viewed as polar opposites but as different manifestations of a

---

[142] Adorno, 'Fetish,' 51.
[143] Ball, *Instinct*, 284 and Meyer, *Emotion*, 32.
[144] Meyer, *Emotion*, 32.
[145] Gabrielsen, 'Brain'.
[146] Ball, *Instinct*, 264.

single psychological process.'[147] Music for ambient listening, which is purely used as a 'mood modifier', or as 'chicken soup for the soul,' as the phrase has it, we must conclude, is reduced to a superficial formula. Devoid of any aesthetic value, music is reduced to a form of self-therapy.[148]

Langer, too, tempers the concept of music as a form of self-expression, 'For the history of music has been a history of more and more integrated, disciplined, and articulated forms, much like the history of language…'[149] She makes the point that 'self-expression requires no artistic form'[150] on the basis that laughter, tears, rage all find expression outside the sphere of music. 'The fact is,' she says, 'that we can use music to work off our subjective experiences and restore our personal balance, but this is not its primary function.'[151]

Therefore, it can easily be concluded that music which articulates nothing but superficial sentiment and is used in this pseudo-cathartic function is lacking in depth and creativity. Good music must surely engage intellect as well as emotion. But the more that recording, digitization and 'ambient listening' dominate our lives, the more detached we become from the music itself.[152] Brian Eno, in discussing his ambient musical compositions, states that it should be as ignorable as it is interesting. He observes, 'We are, in short… increasingly un-centred, un-moored, living day to day, engaged in an ongoing attempt to cobble together a credible, or at least workable, set of values,

---

[147] Meyer, *Emotion*, 39.

[148] Ball, *Instinct*, 271.

[149] Langer, *Philosophy*, 216.

[150] Ibid.

[151] Ibid.

[152] I would include film soundtracks in the 'ambient listening' category. The music enhances dialogue or action – prompting us what to feel, but it is not designed to be a conscious listening experience.

ready to shed it and work out another when the situation demands… gathering experience - the possibility of making better guesses - without demanding certainty.'[153] He acknowledges that his form of music is controversial, 'This… was anathema to those who believe that art should focus our emotions, our higher intelligence, by occupying the centre of attention, lifting us above the mundane environment which burdens our souls.'[154]

Ambient music is to music what illustration is to high art. It is the perfect music for postmodernism, a music of uncertainty and experience, without values, without progress, without demands, reliant purely on mood and the whim of the individual. If, as Susanne Langer states, 'Music doesn't represent emotion so much as mimic it: the ebb and flow of music is analogous to the dynamics of emotion itself,'[155] then in the prevalence of music that expresses little but cheap sentiment rather than real, deep, emotion, we are in danger of becoming so divorced from genuine feeling that we become a nation of psychopaths, able only to produce and use music as little more than an emotional fix.

Creativity

Recording and the preservation of what would otherwise be ephemeral performance has led us into an inexorable cycle of commodification, homogenization, sentimentality and regressive listening. We have seen that for music to be deemed *good* it must engage both intellect and emotion (rather than simple mawkishness), and benefits from *live* performance where the physical presence of the instrumentalist or singer can convey the full power of the piece. A recorded piece of music, produced by a formula

---

[153] Eno, as cited in Toop, *Ocean*, 11.
[154] Ibid., 9.
[155] Langer, as cited in Ball, *Instinct*, 262.

for the sake of economic gain can never convey a true sense of depth.[156]

Technology in music mediates sound - be it speakers, microphones, amplifiers or the recording process. Music technology puts barriers between performer and listener, and produces sound inorganically.[157] The more technology is used, the greater the distance - it would be the projection of an illustration of a copy of a photograph of a painting. Layers upon layers of reproduction and gadgetry strip away the essence of the thing until only the barest utilitarian representation remains. As Ernst Cassirer put it so presciently in 1956, 'Physical reality seems to recede in proportion as man's symbolic activity advances. Instead of dealing with the things themselves man is in a sense constantly conversing with himself. He has so enveloped himself in linguistic forms, in artistic images, in mythical symbols or religious rites that he cannot see or know anything except by the interposition of [an] artificial medium.'[158]

So what does it mean to be truly creative? Do we consider that in order to be valid as an art form, music must be performed in a room with an audience on instruments of wood and bone and gut? Is there no room for the microchip? Cannot technology be creative too?

---

[156] Witness the work of the 'production line' of songs produced out of Tin Pan Alley, New York in the early 20th century, which very much has its equivalent in the later part of the century with the mass-produced music of Stock, Aitken and Waterman and Simon Cowell.

[157] Mathieu, *Listening*, 98.

[158] Cassirer, as cited in Postman, *Amusing*, 11. Cassirer's remark is frighteningly reminiscent of the kind of person who will watch a major event through the electronic eye of their mobile phone camera. Their focus is on the preservation of the moment without actually experiencing the moment for themselves.

Edgard Varèse famously described music as 'organised sound.' This has become a standard definition for many but is, in this context, slightly misleading. Varèse used the term for the first time in describing his own unorthodox and atonal compositions, 'I decided to call my music "organised sound" and myself, *not a musician*, but a "worker in rhythm, frequencies and intensities [italics mine]."'[159] This is someone exploring the extreme edges of what constitutes music, someone who doesn't even consider himself a musician, but a 'worker' - a term more reminiscent of the industrial than the artistic. Perhaps this definition of music is more suited to the contemporary music industry, then. There is no sense of artistry or craftsmanship, only economic value. Musicians under these circumstances become nothing more than 'workers in rhythm, frequencies and intensities.' And the music they produce, however pleasing to the ear, is nothing more than 'organised sound.' As Meyer says, 'The performer is not a musical automaton… [but] a creator who brings to life, through his own sensitivity of feeling and imagination the relationships presented in the musical score…'[160]

Asserting the notion that *industrial/commercial* music is nothing but 'organised sound' separates creativity from the idea that music should be tuneful. Atonal music or music from beyond western culture is creative and, in some ways, more creative than a piece manufactured for its economic worth but to say this is always the case is to be blinkered. Many of the greatest works created during the Italian Renaissance of the 15th century, for example, were made for wealthy patrons such as the Medici of Florence. J.S. Bach, arguably the greatest composer who has ever lived, likewise, wrote and performed for a living. Wilson-Dickson says, 'The overall picture [of Bach's life] is not

---

[159] Varèse, as cited in Ball, *Instinct*, 32.
[160] Meyer, *Emotion*, 199.

one of a creative artist fêted for his prodigious talent. Instead, Bach was regarded as he regarded himself: as a craftsman following in a long family tradition. His task was to glorify God by the composition of music, working to the best of his ability and for a reasonable wage.'[161] So as much as atonal or non-indigenous music is not indicative of a lack of creativity, neither is commerciality. Wilson-Dickson continues, 'It would be a great mistake to imagine that the craftsman-like attitude of Bach, or others in his position, inevitably created well-meaning but arid music. On the contrary, one of Bach's most remarkable talents was his ability to shed new light on a time-worn formula.'[162]

If this elusive concept of *creativity*, then, bears no relation to aesthetic or commercial value perhaps it is connected more to the perception of the one *receiving* the art rather than its purpose in creation. That is to say, something is *creative* if society says it is, much as something is *art* because critical consensus deems it to be so. Now, then, it becomes a question of what we value in music or other artistic forms.

Bennett Reimer provides a long list of reasons why humans value music, among which are,

> ...emotional expression; aesthetic enjoyment; the need to structure reality; the need to share musical experiences and meanings with others; entertainment; spiritual fulfilment; validation and stabilizing of social norms, beliefs and institutions; probing, challenging and changing cultural norms; providing connection with the vast web of humankind over the ages; expanding the

---

[161] Wilson-Dickson, *History*, 158.
[162] Ibid.

> meanings humans are capable of grasping; and on and on
> with values transcending particular times and settings.[163]

This suggests that the true meaning of *creativity* does not lie completely in the simple physical act of making, the originality of an idea, or even an emotional connection to the creation itself. We might consider Mozart a creative genius even though much of his music sits within established musical systems and might be considered formulaic. At the same time, even if we feel no deep, emotional attachment to the music of John Cage, we can appreciate it as *creative* because it challenges the *rules of music* and explores the limits of an accepted definition of *music*. In the cases of both Mozart and Cage, it is not the fact that they went *outside* the rules to create something new, but what they did *within* them, to explore and challenge them.

When we speak of creativity, then, we are speaking of something *made* that goes beyond the superficial, something that might include *spiritual fulfilment* or the challenging and changing of cultural norms. Since Reimer's statement indicates that a worthy value of music is its connection to history and tradition, he is permitting musicians and composers to draw on existing compositional structures. Total originality is not the same as creativity but, at the other extreme, neither is cliché or kitsch.

Creativity then, is about meaning and significance. As Langer says, 'Great art is not a direct sensuous pleasure. If it were, it would appeal - like cake or cocktails - to the untutored as well as to the cultured taste… The artistic idea is always a "deeper" conception.'[164]

---

[163] Reimer, 'Value'.
[164] Langer, *Philosophy*, 205-6.

True creativity values the crafted over the mass-produced; time over speed and efficiency; quality over quantity; the personal over the impersonal; creation or interpretation over reproduction. This is simply because the other side of the coin does not acknowledge anything deeper in a work of art than its simple production. It does not examine concepts like transcendence or spirituality, it does not challenge cultural norms or value the history or tradition of what has gone before. It seeks only to produce rather than to create. True creativity seems to stand in direct opposition to the values of technology and McDonaldization: efficiency, calculability, predictability and control.

Can technology be creative, then? Composer Jonathan Harvey considered that, in writing his 1980 work *Mortuos Plango, Vivos Voco,*

> In entering the rather intimidating world of the machine, I was determined not to produce a dehumanised work if I could help it... The territory that new computer technology opens up is unprecedentedly vast: one is humbly aware that it will only be conquered by penetration of the human spirit, however beguiling the exhibits of technical wizardry; and that penetration will neither be rapid or easy. [165]

Here is one composer using technology to create and yet remaining aware that it has limitations, even dangers. This is where, although it is straightforward to see the creative possibilities, composers and performers must exercise care: that in employing devices and systems to create music we do not lose some sense of humanity in creation. Music is essentially technological - it uses instruments, it works within established forms and musical systems and yet, if McLuhan is to be believed, the medium is the message.

---

[165] Harvey, 'Sketches.'

Therefore, how we use our musical media to create, to perform and to listen, has a profound effect on those activities.

Is the music of Kraftwerk, Jean-Michel Jarre or Terry Riley creative? Undoubtedly. However, in the case of the first, certainly, we can see that they have in some ways submitted themselves to the machine and seem to have sacrificed something of their humanity in the process of creation. Their performances present themselves not as human beings, but as impersonal robots, while their sound is purposefully cold and mechanistic.[166] Meanwhile, the manufactured pop of Stock, Aitken and Waterman, however successful, more closely resembles Varèse's 'organized sound'. It, too, is mechanized but, by contrast, is done without purpose except speed of production for maximum profit. The composers and performers have become 'workers' rather than 'musicians.' So we must reject the accepted definition of music and concur with Scruton when he says,

> We don't make music merely by producing sounds, and… there is indeed a danger, inherent in the very art of music, that it might at any moment collapse into sound - to become a sound effect, whose purpose is to produce responses in something… without drawing our attention to what can be heard and imagined in the rhythmic and melodic line.[167]

It is humanity and its expression that makes music *music*. What then becomes of the listener who is constantly exposed to commercialized *non-music*? Do they also not sacrifice something of their humanity?[168] Are they

---

[166] In mainstream pop, this style of 'robotic' performance is echoed by performers such as Daft Punk.

[167] Scruton, 'Soul'.

[168] Does one truly become less human by listening to piped music? Leave aside that one doesn't *listen* to piped music, one has it played *at*

consumed by the machine as much as they are consumers? Are they irrevocably changed by their listening?

Eisler and Adorno suggest that commercial and mechanized music serves simply to distract listeners from the harsh realities of life. 'Put into the service of commercialism... music can be made to serve regression... and in that role is more welcomed in proportion as it deceives its listeners in regard to the reality of everyday existence.'[169]

All of which, of course, begs another question. If music should serve a 'higher purpose,' if it is more than simply 'mood modification,' or self-expression, then what should that purpose be?

Purpose

Langer rejects the concept of music and the arts as 'self-expression', as we have already seen. However, she does not dismiss the fact that music taps into the reservoir of human emotion. She says, 'The arts objectify subjective reality, and subjectify outward experience of nature. Art education is the education of feeling, and a society that neglects it gives itself up to formless emotion.'[170] She continues, 'Art is craftsmanship, but to a special end: the creation of expressive forms...that set forth the nature of human feeling.'[171] In other words, music and other art-forms give form to emotion and lived experience. The creation of art is not an expression of self, as such, but an

---

you, consider the logic that if music expresses our creative humanity and deserves our full attention, then piped music, and the lackadaisical attitudes towards music that emerge from its ubiquity, must, logically, devalue our humanness. That this seems extreme and unpalatable, does not make it any less true.

[169] Eisler and Adorno, 'Politics'.

[170] Langer, *Problems*, 74.

[171] Ibid., 111.

expression of our very humanity and music gives form not only to those things that we express as human beings but also to those things that are inexpressible any other way.

Once asked what his 3rd symphony meant, Beethoven sat down at the piano and began to play it.[172] The music meant what it meant, it was not representative of something that could be expressed in any other form. As Isadora Duncan is reputed to have said, 'If I could tell you what it meant, there would be no point in dancing it.'[173]

> Music is revealing, where words are obscuring, because it can have not only a content, but a transient play of contents. It can articulate feelings without becoming wedded to them… The assignment of meanings is a shifting, kaleidoscopic play, probably below the threshold of consciousness, certainly outside the pale of discursive thinking.[174]

Scruton, meanwhile, contends that music and the arts has a moral quality all of its own. It reveals what we value. 'Aesthetic interest does not stem from our passing desires; it reveals what we are and what we value. Taste, like style, is the man himself.'[175] This implies that if we value the superficial; if we chase after celebrity for its own sake rather than for any cultural accomplishment; if we are not critical of those forms of art with which we come into contact; then our culture and identity is shaped both as individuals and as a nation to become like it. Criticism, Scruton proposes,

> …is a last ditch attempt to be part of the artistic tradition, to retain the internal perspective on an inherited culture, and to fight off the corruption of

---

[172] Ball, *Instinct*, 387.
[173] Duncan, as quoted in Astley et al, *Chords*, xiv.
[174] Langer, *Philosophy*, 243.
[175] Scruton, *Culture*, 35.

sentiment that comes about, when cliché and sentimentality are mistaken for sincere expression. By eliciting sympathy towards empty forms, the cliché impoverishes the emotional life of those who are drawn to it.[176]

Key above any emotional or moral value to music and art in general must be the way it connects us to the spiritual. As painter Wassily Kandinsky says, 'The spiritual life, to which art belongs and of which she is one of the mightiest elements, is a complicated but definite and easily definable movement forwards and upwards. This movement is the movement of experience. It may take different forms, but it holds at bottom to the same inner thought and purpose.'[177]

For the Christian, this is an easy connection to make. As God creates mankind in his own image (Gen 1:26) so mankind in turn has the power to create and because music is capable of expressing what is otherwise inexpressible, it provides the perfect vehicle for relating to God. The music itself does not even need be, what today we would describe as, *Christian music*. Indeed, to create a split between *secular* and *sacred* is poor theology. As Philip Phenix says, 'By definition, God is the ultimate standard for anything and everything. Nothing is irrelevant to him and no affair of life falls outside religious concern.'[178] An omniscient, omnipotent and omnipresent God encompasses the whole of existence, so to limit God to the *sacred* is to deny his involvement in the whole of life. Does this mean, then, that all art, has a spiritual quality? Phenix continues,

---

[176] Scruton, *Culture*, 45.
[177] Kandinsky, *Concerning*, 4.
[178] Phenix, *Education*, 18.

Not every work of art is a manifestation of the work of God. Some experiences in the arts are edifying and some are not. Some predominate in spiritual power; others are either vacuous or demonic. Some works help people become more perfectly related to their spiritual ground and thus to become more completely themselves; others are instruments of self-negation and alienation.[179]

Even what we might term *ugly art* - objects or music with which we find a connection difficult - can have a spiritual quality, albeit a negative one. Some *ugly art* might even serve to remind us of our imperfections as human beings and draw us away from the fallen and distorted nature of creation towards the perfection of God. Therefore, art of any nature is rooted in the reality of the world as it is, but lifts our eyes to the possibility of something better, towards redemption, towards God. However, as Brand and Chaplin warn, 'Art can create a longing for God or an awareness of God, but it cannot give us a life lived under God.'[180]

Conclusion

We have seen from this chapter that music has become increasingly subject to the demands of the technological world with its devices and systems. Reproductive technology, be it stave or studio, means that music is no longer the fleeting, evanescent creation that it once was. The preservation of certain performances has led, in turn to the commodification of music and, through the consequent demands of the listener, to its homogenization. Through the desire for 'mood modification' and music that serves as a soundtrack to everyday life, or as a distraction from it, commercialized music seeks to move the emotions

---

[179] Phenix, *Education*, 97.
[180] Brand & Chaplin, *Art*, 89.

in a superficial, sentimental fashion rather than engaging in depth of feeling.

This is not to say that all commercial music is like this, nor that musicians are not entitled to make money from their art. It is simply to say that we are, in pursuing this line, in danger of cutting off music from certain themes, limiting our composition to a stock set of melodic, harmonic and rhythmic tropes[181] and damaging our ability to accept music, or indeed other art, that does not conform to these types. Our human creativity suffers when we allow machines to make our music - even to the extent that we validate music created entirely by machine.[182]

Are there positives to the use of digital technology in the creation of music? Undoubtedly, the recording process allows us to preserve historically significant performances and allows us to become exposed to music from around the world that would otherwise be unknown to us. For the listener, there are increasing ways of consuming music. The live performance, vinyl, CD, TV or Internet-based music streaming services all allow us to access a huge range of recordings from all around the world if only, in the case of the latter, we can break free of the algorithms that dictate what we will like and allow ourselves to be challenged by the unfamiliar.

In composition, programmes such as Logic and Garageband make it easier than ever for people with ability and talent to realize their creative dreams. Not only is it easier, it is also substantially quicker and cheaper to use a synthesized string section on a computer than it is to hire a studio and employ a string orchestra. That being said, of course, the home studio can destroy the concept of

---

[181] Percino et al., 'Complexity'.
[182] Ball, 'Iamus'.

making music as a communal activity. There is no relationship between composer and performer because they are one and the same - one person and a keyboard can create the sound of a complete orchestra or rock band. The employment of loops and samples only adds to a sense of homogenization. Even a genuine orchestra can be made into something artificial. As W. Brian Arthur states, 'A live symphony can be brought "down" into electronics world via microphone equipment, manipulated there - processed electronically and recorded, say - and brought back "up and out" again when it enters the physical world again to be played as sound.'[183]

For the performer, the use of microphones and amplification allows them to reach large, live audiences in huge arenas. It allows them to manipulate sound through the use of effects, should they wish. Even classical music concerts may have microphones to *balance* the sound of the orchestra - to amplify the sound of the strings over the brass section, for example. What harm can there be in making music louder? Volume can flatten the sound of music to the extent that there is no longer any sense of dynamics, disrupting the internal rhythm of a piece - that is any sense of tension and release - upon which good composition relies. Instead, music is played *at* us, a wall of sound that creates a barrier rather than an invitation to engage *with* the music itself, while silence becomes a virtual impossibility.

Music in the 21st century has become the market. Certainly for popular forms, since the rise of MTV and television stations like them, music has become less about depth of composition, arrangement or quality of performance than it has about image and marketability. The danger of this is that as music of this nature becomes more and more

---

[183] Arthur, *Nature*, 81.

prevalent, to the exclusion of other forms or of other cultures; as our musical tastes become, perversely, more and more limited even as our ability to access music becomes greater and greater, we risk sacrificing musical quality without even any realization that we are doing so.

For the Christian church and the music we use, this has profound implications. It means we seek potentially to amuse and entertain rather than to declare the truth of God together, and place individual satisfaction over discipleship and love of neighbour. 'If how we worship shapes what we believe, then it is imperative that we pay attention to how we worship. If worship is shaped by culture, it will result in culturally conditioned faith. If worship is shaped by narcissism, it will result in a me-oriented consumer faith.'[184]

Consider, then, what has been asserted thus far:

-    The purpose of music is as a 'tonal analogue'[185] to emotional life.
-    Music lifts us beyond ourselves and connects us to each other, to wider creation and even to God.
-    Our aesthetic judgments carry a moral value in shaping how we think and feel.
-    'The medium is message,' – the manner in which we access music determines the limits of how we perceive it, and of what music we are able to create for ourselves and future generations.

If we admit these to be true, then how music and technology interact within our churches - our *sacred spaces* - is going to be critical to determining how we perceive God, how we develop our theology, the things that we

---

[184] Webber, *Worship*, 104.
[185] Langer, *Feeling*, 27.

value and the things that we do not, and how we connect to each other as a community of believers.

It will even define what we mean by *community* itself.

3

TECHNOLOGY, MUSIC AND THE CHURCH

The Church knew what the psalmist knew: Music praises God.
Music is well or better able to praise him than the building of the
church and all its decoration; it is the Church's greatest ornament.
— Igor Stravinsky

Let us accept that 'the medium is the message' - that is, all the devices and systems we employ accentuate and augment particular aspects of our life and character, permitting certain activities and prohibiting others, thereby shaping our culture and society. Since we have seen this in action specifically in the world of music and the arts, it does not take the greatest of leaps to conclude that the technology and music we use in our churches has a profound impact in the formation of our theology and on our expressions of corporate worship.

This is not an issue of positivity or negativity - we are not seeking to say that non-technological is A Good Thing while anything technological is A Bad Thing.[186] As we have

---

[186] W.C. Sellar & R.J. Yeatman, '1066 and All That'.

already seen, music is inherently technological, in that it operates within certain systems however much those systems are acknowledged. The *purest, non-technological* music would be one that employs the unaccompanied voice as some churches, such as the Quakers or Primitive Baptists, do even to this day.[187] But even here, churches that use nothing but the voice are still working within basic musical structures and so are, as such, employing a technology. This means that technology within corporate worship is both a question of conscious employment, and a question of degree. The issue at hand, then, becomes not whether we should or should not employ technology, but rather the extent to which we should employ it while ensuring that we address questions concerning its impact. These are the themes that we will seek to examine in this chapter.

A Brief Definition of Worship

Before we proceed further, it is important that we clarify what we mean by the term *worship*. One of the best overall definitions of the word comes from David Peterson who states that 'worship of the living and true God is essentially an engagement with him on the terms that he proposes and in the way that he alone makes possible.'[188] His reasoning is based on separating the concept of *worship* from the experiential. He asks, 'Are there special moments within a Christian meeting when we are truly "worshipping" God? Are church services to be measured by the extent to which they enable the participants to enter into such experiences?'[189] He concludes that worship is far more than a hyped sense of emotional or spiritual self-gratification and that, scripturally, *worship* encompasses an

---

[187] The Primitive Baptists give their reasoning for not using instruments at www.pb.org/pbdocs/music. An internet search for 'churches using unaccompanied voice' yields plenty of other examples.
[188] Peterson, *Engaging*, 20.
[189] Ibid., 16.

overall attitude of service and submission in obedience to God's commandments to love him and to love our neighbour, 'responding appropriately to God's own self-revelation.'[190]

'Acceptable worship,' Peterson states, 'is an engagement with God, through Jesus Christ, in the Holy Spirit - a Christ-centred, gospel-serving, life-orientation.'[191] He is concerned to distance the concept of worship from a limited corporate expression which he considers has more to do with the mutual edification of the church than it does with any mystical experience.[192]

Although Peterson's definition provides us with great biblical accuracy, and reflects the way we *should* talk about worship, it does not necessarily reflect the way we *actually* talk about worship, particularly in the context of the gathered church. Most of the time, when the word *worship* is mentioned, it is usually connected to the music and liturgy of a Sunday service. A leader will invite the congregation to stand 'as we move into a time of worship' after the welcome and notices. Perhaps a church might have a tautologous 'time of praise and worship,' which limits the concept of worship still further to slow tempo, reflective songs as opposed to upbeat 'praise' songs.

When did worship stop being the umbrella term for our whole life response to the love of God and start being confined to music? Is it possible that the technology we employ in our gatherings makes it difficult to conceive of a definition of worship that extends beyond the walls of the church? This is a significant question, as it means that our ability to create true community and to form relationships necessary to God's mission for the church, is hindered by

---

[190] Peterson, *Engaging*, 170.
[191] Ibid., 293.
[192] Ibid., 206-221.

the very tools we employ in seeking to make church more relevant to contemporary society.

So this is where our definition of worship must sit, despite its theological inadequacies - within the corporate expression of devotion to God and when *worship* is mentioned in this chapter, it will invariably be in that context unless otherwise noted.

Worship, Recording & Commodification

It is possible to trace the use of popular musical forms within corporate worship as far back as Martin Luther, and some see his ready marriage of the folk melodies of the day to lyrics appropriate for congregational singing as the start of a slippery slope towards the *dumbing down* of church music.[193] But as Andrew Wilson-Dickson states, Luther was familiar with Gregorian chant and was not only a trained singer but also a skilled lutenist. As such, he took a very high view of music's potential power over the emotions.[194] 'Luther's fundamental desire that Christians should worship God with sincerity and understanding did not mean that he wished to abandon the Latin Mass.'[195]

In actuality, Luther stands apart from some of his contemporaries[196] in that he did not seek to restrict the use of music but sought to use it to proclaim the gospel in an authentic and immediately intelligible way. As someone who had a great appreciation of music's aesthetic, ethical and affective power, he understood that there was a level of appropriateness in musical choices, 'insisting on

---

[193] This is despite the fact that the phrase, "Why should the devil have all the best tunes?" is not something that can be attributed to Luther with any degree of certainty according to Begbie.

[194] Wilson-Dickson, *History*, 93.

[195] Ibid.

[196] Especially John Calvin.

material that was crafted and durable.'[197] To this end, in the Lutheran tradition, *high* music sat alongside popular, folk music.

By the nineteenth century revivalist movement, figures such as William Booth and Moody and Sankey, were keen to employ 'gospel songs that had the ability to reach large numbers powerfully and effectively with a simple message.'[198] In doing so, Booth particularly, looked on professional choirs with a degree of suspicion, preferring the use of a solo voice, 'Merely professional music,' he said, 'is always a curse and should you ever find a choir in connection with any hall or mission, I give you my authority to… sweep it out, promising that you do so as lovingly as possible.'[199] Wilson-Dickson contends that, 'the frank emotionalism of these songs and their imitation or borrowing of secular pop music for their purposes was offensive to more aesthetically-minded observers'[200] and there grew an ever-increasing chasm between *art music* and *church music*. According to Wilson-Dickson,

> In all this the losers were - and to a certain extent still are - the established churches. Their traditions of musical excellence were deprived of the stimulus of truly inventive minds by the churches' rejection of full-blooded Romanticism. What Christians were left with was a diluted and anodyne modern music which gained diminishing respect and attention from the educated public.[201]

The rise of popular music forms in the twentieth century, however, owes little to this history. Neither is it necessarily connected to a desire to make the church culturally

---

[197] Begbie, *Resounding*, 100-1.
[198] Wilson-Dickson, *History*, 231.
[199] Booth as quoted in Wilson-Dickson, *History*, 234.
[200] Wilson-Dickson, *History*, 234.
[201] Ibid., 237.

relevant. It is, in actuality, born out of perfectly natural progress: new Christians joining the church in the 1960s and '70s brought with them the musical forms with which they were familiar.

Many churches struggled to keep pace with this younger generation, though, and were unable to produce the necessary resources, until companies like Kingsway set about creating the songbooks that were so desperately needed. Ward suggests that the first attempt to bring the music of pop culture and church together was in the 1966 publication of *Youth Praise*. This, he suggests, 'involved a cultural logic of media related production and consumption that was to change the dominant cultural pattern within evangelicalism.'[202] One suspects that he is somewhat overstating the case. The more measured assessment of Wilson-Dickson indicates that 'the contents…betrayed the musical interests of its adult compilers and bore little relation to the secular youth music of the time (the Beatles, the Rolling Stones).'[203] That being said, it does seem to mark the beginning of a gradual increase in production of popular songbooks all the way from *Psalm Praise* to *Mission Praise* and *Songs of Fellowship*. Since its first publication in the early 1980s, the latter has spawned five substantial volumes to date. The printed songbook, however, appears to be in terminal decline as a resource faced, as it is, with stiff competition from internet- and computer-based resources such as *worshiptogether.com* (owned by EMI), *OnSong* and *SongSelect*.

Meanwhile, the development of festivals such as *Spring Harvest* and *New Wine* have provided a select group of worship songwriters with a platform to present their music. In the excited atmosphere of a large conference, it

---

[202] Ward, *Selling*, 27.
[203] Wilson-Dickson, *History*, 412.

is unsurprising that they find a willing, captive market, keen to recreate the *worship experience* on a local level. Consequently, the albums and songbooks that are produced provide a resource to churches, who use the songs and increasing amounts of electronic gear in an attempt to create the *feel* of the conference. 'The point,' according to Ward, 'is that a mediated religious culture makes the product widely available and once commodified it can be reinterpreted and reshaped by location and context.'[204] In this way *worship music* has swiftly become the *worship music industry*.

In embracing the culture of production based on popular music, worship music has gradually become as commodified as its secular counterpart.[205] Ward sees the commodification of ministry and the growth of the *worship business* as an inevitable consequence of the 'contextualisation of faith within popular culture.'[206] It is not difficult to deduce, therefore, that in placing corporate worship within that environment, the issues surrounding secular music now also surround contemporary Christian worship music.

Pop music forms use a *product* formula for distribution. This means that songs reach churches through events and merchandising, through CDs and, increasingly, via the Internet. The same can be said of the Christian music sub-culture. However, when products are released through reputable Christian companies, there is an inbuilt expectation of musical and theological integrity that does not necessarily exist in the nature of the form. 'Pop [the worship song] brings with it its own views of the lyric. In poetry [the hymn], what matters is the words… In pop

---

[204] Ward, *Selling*, 72.
[205] Ibid., 70.
[206] Ibid., 95.

songs what matters is the melody, the hook, the beat. Having decent lyrics is a bonus.'[207]

According to Peterson, 'We do not gather simply for the spiritual uplift we may experience, but to encourage one another to be outward looking, to care for our neighbours, our society and our world.'[208] But the commodification of worship means that we are creating music that seeks to satisfy our own wants and needs, that speaks to our own desires, however noble they may be. It is the commodification of worship that leads to people leaving churches because 'the worship doesn't speak to me.' It is the commodification of worship that leads to the so-called worship wars, as worship becomes limited to musical, stylistic choices and 'spiritual uplift' rather than a deeper engagement with God and with each other. Marva Dawn suggests that,

> Not only is the idea of taste as an entry point [into a congregation] wrong biblically, but also it is extremely destructive of genuine community, fosters an independent view of the local congregation, and reduces worship simply to a matter of preferences instead of an entering into God's presence in the company of the Church throughout space and time.[209]

In reality, the *worship wars* are inevitable if we see worship as a product, because products are necessarily targeted to particular markets, and different markets must compete to survive.

Commodification also brings with it disposability and a planned obsolescence. When the object of a commodity is to make money for an organization, whatever its purpose,

---

207 Page, *Nonsense*, 37.
208 Peterson, *Encountering*, 62.
209 Dawn, *Waste*, 187.

then there is a constant need to change and develop. This leads to a constant need to *upgrade* regardless of whether the object performs its function adequately already. The mobile telephone is a perfect example of this. In the commodified worship music industry, the ephemeral nature of the pop song is eminently suited to a fast pace of change in order to ensure the economic future of the business. It would be fair to say that some songs even from the turn of the 21st century would, in 2015, be considered old. Interestingly, there seem to be very few songs from the 1980s, compared to the volume produced, that continue to be popular today[210] and, arguably, most of those that do survive have what might be considered a hymn-like structure.[211]

The sheer speed and quantity of output means that many churches struggle to keep up with the newest songs, or are in a constant state of newness - learning new songs even before the older ones have had a chance become a regular part of their corporate worship life. As Page puts it, 'We have a church that is addicted to newness, part of a culture which worship continuous consumption, and in the pop song we have found the perfect model for the easy-come, easy-go worship song.'[212]

Because we use *worship music* in the same way we use any other music - to be played on radio stations; to be quantified in sales charts; to be experienced as ambient listening as a wholesome alternative to *secular* music; to try

---

[210] One-third of the top 25 according to CCLI's Church Copyright Licence Top 25. *Be Still* (1986), *There Is A Redeemer* (1982), *Shine, Jesus Shine* (1987), *The Servant King* (1983), *Faithful One* (1989), *All Heaven Declares* (1987), *Lord I Lift Your Name On High* (1989) and *As the Deer* (1984) are all still regularly used in congregational worship as at January 2015. The highest entry is *Be Still* at number 3.

[211] This is not necessarily an argument in favour of the hymn, as we shall see.

[212] Page, *Nonsense*, 39.

and preserve the *live* experience and spiritual high of the conference through recordings, it is not surprising that record labels see *worship music* as just another sector of the wider music industry, placed alongside pop, rock and rave music as just another niche to be exploited.

As a consequence, in a society where music has become so ubiquitous, musical choices have come to dominate our understanding of church - worship leaders apparently choose songs determined by the latest conference or concert, by what they hear on Christian radio, or on CDs such as *The Best Worship Songs… Ever!* and its follow-up *More… Best Worship Songs… Ever!*[213] It is simply a logical extension, then, to suggest that all this, in turn, not only affects the aesthetic sensibilities of the congregation but also shapes their theology. Robert Webber sounds an eloquent warning, 'If how we worship shapes what we believe, then it is imperative that we pay attention to how we worship. If worship is shaped by culture, it will result in culturally conditioned faith. If worship is shaped by narcissism, it will result in a me-oriented consumer faith.'[214]

Worship, Performance & Homogenization

As we have seen with recordings of other music, worship albums have an impact on *live* performance. For many churches, the conference provides the epitome of what worship is perceived to be and so spend a great deal of time and money trying to replicate it. Rather than trying to interpret songs for the local context, using the resources they have available, some churches choose to focus their effort on trying to recreate the conference experience in their Sunday services, and replicate the arrangements of

---

[213] Both from EMI, who should be ashamed of themselves, for appalling grammar if nothing else.
[214] Webber, *Worship*, 104.

songs heard on whichever CD happens to be the most popular. This is often done without the conscious knowledge that they are endeavouring to recreate a sound that may be entirely a studio construct. But while the desire for high production values and musical excellence is commendable, it creates nothing more than a slick, professional performance divorcing the context of the musicians from that of the congregation. Furthermore, in order to recreate a particular atmosphere, some churches will invest in screens, in microphones and powerful PA systems, in coloured lights and even dry ice machines. This in turn leads to further dislocation between musicians and congregation, as the worship becomes mediated through the technology employed and erects not just a sonic barrier but also, in some cases, a physical one.

In mediating worship, we are in danger of creating the impression that all that matters are the numbers of people present, since there is little that distinguishes attendance at church and attendance at a concert. If, as churches, we import pop music's commercial, target-driven culture, focusing on nothing except that which is quantifiable, then spiritual growth and integrity will become stunted and, ultimately, undermined. As a consequence, the message of the gospel becomes substituted for one that essentially focuses on trends and statistics, or as Detweiler states, 'Followers of Jesus must deal with the cultural perception that the institutionalized church has reduced religion to hamburgers.'[215]

Marketing and product-placement play a significant part in the contemporary worship music scene. The music and performers are packaged, promoted and sold in much the same way as their secular pop counterparts.[216] In the same

---

[215] Detweiler, *Matrix*, 131.
[216] Ward, *Selling*, 184.

way that secular music has substituted content for image, the rise of the *rock star worship leader* is in danger of becoming idolatry. According to Liesch, 'The reality is...people are attracted in great numbers to hear the good performers, the skilled speakers and musicians. We are inclined to buy into the entertainment syndrome and exalt the Christian performer, preacher or musician. This ought to make us uneasy.'[217] The celebrity worship leader has become the new priesthood, with technology the tool of their mediation.

Again, we must be careful not to denigrate a desire for quality and excellence that seeks to give to God the very best that we are able. But with a pre-packaged, mechanistic, image-driven form of worship comes a programmatic and rationalistic mindset, that controls and limits creativity to a success-driven formula defined by attendance and atmosphere.

According to Ward, although worship music is central to organizations like Soul Survivor, contemporary forms of music are not used as an attempt to attract young people. Neither is it driven by a feeling that church should be trendy in some way.[218] Their use of music is based on their theology of worship in which encounter with God by the Holy Spirit is mediated through song.[219] 'This means that the various merchandise of CDs, songbooks, festivals, magazines and the websites were run in the belief that these products and services were 'resources' which helped young people meet with God.'[220]

Local congregations look at the apparent success of organizations such as Hillsong or Soul Survivor and

---

[217] Liesch, *Worship*, 122.
[218] Ward, *Selling*, 106.
[219] And by association, through technology.
[220] Ward, *Selling*, 107.

endeavour to recreate the formula in an inappropriate context, failing to take into account the communities within which they are placed. At the same time, Hillsong, who epitomize this kind of programme mentality, even go so far as to encourage it by the creation of a 'Global Project' that exports their musical style to the world and effectively homogenizes worship music.[221]

Because record labels like EMI are concerned with sustaining a profitable business rather than the spiritual wellbeing of congregations, they encourage - as they do with any other form of music - a successful formula which ensures sales. Consequently, melodic and harmonic lines, chord progressions and styles become restricted to that which is already successful - we undergo Adorno's 'regression of listening' and the music we employ in our Sunday services becomes ever more limited. This also includes lyrical limitations, as certain theological themes like lament or imprecation are not likely to be successful in selling albums. Therefore, we are left with nothing but upbeat, relentlessly cheerful or sentimentally devotional music that fails to speak to the realities of Christian life. Consequently, not only has our sense of the aesthetic in music become stunted and distorted, so too has our theology.

A church focused on programmes and formulae fails to take into account the needs of the congregation and wider community and impairs genuine, deep relationship. Any negative emotion, doubt or spiritual search becomes repressed on the basis that it doesn't fit the overall scheme. Drane states that 'we have come to value one another mostly in mechanistic terms related to production and output... The way Western culture has developed in the last two hundred years or so is that daily life is no longer

---

[221] See *www.hillsongglobalproject.com* for examples of this.

carried out in a relational context.'[222] As secular music is used as a means of coping with work so church music, too, fails to represent the real world in which people live and work compromising our authenticity as human beings working out our faith in society. 'Christians will fulfill their calling by guarding the integrity of the right questions, rather than handing out slick answers.'[223]

The relational aspect of corporate worship also suffers when a church obsessed with all things new loses its connection to the past. White maintains that 'Since the maintaining of tradition…depends upon a meaningful continuity of past and present, tradition… breaks down with the increasing fragmentation of time and experience, which technological society intensifies.'[224] For a corporate spiritual life that requires a significant investment of time, attentiveness and effort there is a danger that the values of a digital world are incompatible.[225] According to our earlier definition, true creativity roots itself in tradition and humanity. Rather than looking forward to *the next big thing*, then, perhaps churches would be better served by looking back and recapturing a sense of history. 'If our worship is not costly in terms of time, participation and commitment, how will we teach what discipleship means? The medium must match the message.'[226]

Worship, Mood & Emotion

The emotional atmosphere of the conference has led churches to confuse the affective power of music with worship. Should worship be an emotional experience? Of course emotions play their part as we express our love of

---

[222] Drane, *McDonaldization*, 20.
[223] Ibid., 38.
[224] White, *Change*, 22.
[225] Ibid., 112.
[226] Dawn, *Waste*, 61.

and dedication to God, but in many cases 'times of worship are judged, not on whether people were changed or challenged or renewed, but on the response of the crowd, the 'buzz' in the building. This is not a reliable indicator of the presence of God.'[227] While we seem to have pulled back from the overtly romantic intimacy that expressed itself in some of the songs of the '80s and '90s to a more balanced and theologically educated approach seen in the work of writers like Matt Redman, Stuart Townend and the Gettys, there remains a sense, still, that worship is deemed successful by the heartstrings it tugs, or by *the sense of God's presence* - which seems to be indicated by an indefinable sense of bliss - as if God were somehow more present in worship than he might be somewhere else.

Rather than embracing creative variety, many churches have reduced their worship music to a popular culture stream, modelling Adorno's regression of listening. This causes the diet of music and emotional expression to become reduced to 'mood modification.' Consequently, congregations begin to equate worship with sentimentality and emotional affectiveness. Worship leaders may even elect and discard songs on this basis.[228] Worship, if we can call it that, becomes merely a form of self-therapy. One blog equates it to a cocaine rush, citing a case of a woman who went from conference to conference seeking the 'euphoric "oomph."'[229] The author goes on to observe that 'Worship rush-seeking is simply another instance of this intense concentration on the self. We fail to recognize its self-centeredness because it's disguised as "worship."'[230]

Many who are drawn to seek an emotional high, rather than the glory of God and transformation into the likeness

---

[227] Page, *Nonsense*, 42.
[228] Nicol, 'Lifecycle'.
[229] Williamson, 'Cocaine'.
[230] Ibid.

of Christ, are not satisfied that they have worshipped until they have been moved emotionally. Marva Dawn says, 'We permit [worship to be market driven] when we study what the consumers/worship participants fancy more than we study what is right with God! Then worship, too, becomes pseudo-therapy and not the healing revelation of God.'[231]

Music, however, has always been a question of tension and release, so it is not necessary to consider the affective power of music to be something that is inherently sinful or wrong in any way. Composers of all kinds of music use certain musical devices to create particular effects, for example, 'While the trained musician consciously waits for the expected resolution of a dominant seventh chord the untrained, but practiced, listener feels the delay as affect.'[232] Is this manipulative? To a degree, certainly, since the composer of the piece wishes us to respond in a particular way to their composition. These kind of musical devices are consciously employed so that the listener experiences the sense of what the composer wants to convey, and music as a 'tonal analogue of emotive life'[233] would have no power or meaning otherwise. As Calvin has said, 'Should the Lord have attracted our eyes to the beauty of the flowers, and our senses to pleasant odours… and should it be a sin to drink them in?… Has he not made many things worthy of our attention that go far beyond our needs?'[234]

But we need to understand and recognize the difference between the transience of *mood* against deeply felt and embedded *emotion*. Mood, which shifts in the passing of the day, is entirely based on circumstance and individual felt need. Emotion has an intellectual quality that reaches to

---

[231] Dawn, *Reaching*, 24.
[232] Meyer, *Emotion*, 40.
[233] Langer, *Feeling*, 27.
[234] Calvin as quoted in Brand & Chaplin, *Art*, 31.

the core of our humanity. 'Inspiration is not sentimentality. Ecstasy is not merely a gush of emotion; mere sentiment is an irrational form of excitation that does not contribute to the fulfilment of humanness.'[235] Or as Scruton puts it,

> Sentimental feeling is easy to confuse with the real thing, for, on the surface at least, they have the same object... But this superficial similarity marks a deep difference. The real focus of my sentimental love is... me. For the sentimentalist it is not the object but the subject of emotion that is important. Real love focuses on the other: it is gladdened by his pleasure and grieved by his pain. The unreal love of the sentimentalist focuses on the self, and treats the pleasures and pains of its object only as an excuse for playing the role that most appeals to it... For secretly sentimentalists welcome the sorrow that prompts their tears. It is another excuse for the noble gesture, another occasion to contemplate the image of a great-hearted self.[236]

How can we tell when our worship of God is descending into the sentimental? In practice we must notice when it values our own feelings above everything, that when we sing 'It's all about you' we really mean 'it's all about me' and how it makes me feel. It is when we allow this pseudo-therapeutic form of corporate worship to dominate, that worship enters the realms of entertainment rather than encounter. We must not confuse the affective power of music, through compositional or dynamic devices with the presence of God. The Holy Spirit indwells the believer and God is always present whether we *feel* it or not. What changes when music is performed, is our awareness of that presence and our sense of connection to the transcendent. The music changes *us*, not God.

---

[235] Phenix, *Education*, 96.
[236] Scruton, *Culture*, 64.

Good and true worship, then, will enable us to give an emotional response to an intellectual and spiritual understanding – the quality of our worship will be found in the depth of our theology. It is not mindless repetition or emotional manipulation, it is not focused on ourselves, but it is centred on the realization of who God is and what he has accomplished for us in Christ.

Worship, Tools & Technology

Does all this mean, then, that we should abandon contemporary forms of worship music and revert to the *good old days* of the hymn and harmonium? Can popular worship music forms express deep emotion, or are they mired in sentimentality?

To suggest that in order to create *true* worship we must return to the hymnal is as false a statement as to say that we should abandon the hymnal for purely contemporary forms of worship - these two stances forming the extreme ends of the so-called 'worship wars'. Personal preference, be it for hymn or pop song, still remains a means of selecting music based on individual taste. This lies at the heart of the 'worship must speak to me' mentality that sees so many individuals commute to large churches on industrial estates - the church equivalent of the out-of-town shopping mall - rather than seeking to worship as part of their immediate local community.

One of the most common arguments for the use of technology within the church is that it permits a greater degree of creativity than the *hymn sandwich* form of church service. Microphones and multimedia allow us to do things that we would not be able to do otherwise. This is certainly true. The microphone amplifies the voice and allows the drama of offstage speech. Disembodied voices narrate a story or a dramatized Bible passage, or perhaps an electronic effect changes vocal pops and clicks into the sound of drums. Or perhaps it is simply used to fill a bigger hall. At the heart of the latter use is a church that values numbers. It sees successful worship as a matter of quantity rather than quality. It can also be, and has been, argued that a larger church makes it harder for individuals to build up proper, deep and lasting relationships. This, then, would run counter to a broader definition of worship that sees the edification of the congregation and the needs of others as a prime reason for meeting together. Does this make the microphone wrong? Is amplification a sin? Of course not! But it becomes evident that the microphone permits some creative use in performance while taking away something deeper in terms of relationships and quality of spiritual life and growth. As Ward says, 'Sound systems are mediators of the music. They transmit the music, but as they do so they affect the way that it is presented and experienced.'[237]

The solution? This depends on the context of the individual church and congregation. But it may be worth considering that smaller congregations spread over more geographical locations allow the church to reach more of the community of which they have been called to be a part. The microphone, in this context, could very well be said to be hindering the growth of the church, since we consider a large central location to be better suited to *worship* than to be spread out in the midst of local communities. Redefining worship as something that builds up others rather than the *warm fuzzies* will naturally lead to a more missionally-minded church. Being smaller, churches will be better suited to create forms of corporate worship that speak to their immediate context and because the church plants have strong connections to their wider surroundings, there is greater possibility of networking,

---

[237] Ward, *Selling*, 90.

cooperation and mutual support. We can conclude that a single church of 300+ members, made viable by technology, may well reach fewer people than six churches of 50 active, growing and mature Christians.

What of the video screen? Surely the creative possibilities there are endless?

> In churches, especially fast-growing charismatic and mega churches, visual and dramatic arts are becoming a standard part of worship. Special effects, dramatic skits, movie clips, slides of artwork, to say nothing of worship bands, are common in "contemporary" worship services. While some may doubt whether these works and compositions will stand the test of time, or whether they are contributing to truly biblical worship, clearly there is creative energy - an excitement - here.[238]

As a replacement for the printed book, there are some positives. Congregations now have freedom of movement, their eyes are lifted from the page to look around them and become aware of their surroundings and of the people with whom they are gathered. The drawbacks, however, may require the church to be darkened, because the projector isn't strong enough to display clearly in bright sunshine. The screen might display a countdown to the start of the service, which serves only to remind people of the passage of time, creating a clock-watching congregation that seeks only to leave in order to get on with the more important work of daily life. It might also display a video that the congregation can sit and watch passively, as they would do the TV at home. Finally, a dark church defeats the object of releasing people from the hymnbook in the first place, since they are unable to look around and connect with others in the service, or interact with their sacred space - assuming that such a church

---

[238] Dyrness, *Visual*, 14.

building has any architectural or artistic worth from which a worshiper may derive meaning.

It would seem that a church dependent on the screen need not bother meeting together for all the interaction that takes place. Yet, we live in a visual culture. 'The contemporary generation has been raised and nourished by images; it has an inescapably visual imagination… For this generation, aesthetics counts more than epistemology.'[239] For us not to use video or photographic technology in corporate worship seems counter-intuitive. But once again, we must be conscious of what this technology emphasizes and how it affects our church culture. 'As the meaning of music lies in what is does rather than what it represents, so with visual art it can be said that its significance lies in what it does with what it represents.'[240] Television and video screens may allow us to visualize difficult concepts - a picture is worth a thousand words, they say. They connect the church to the world outside, but it is a world of frenetic pace, of flashing and flashy visuals that move, sometimes too fast for the eye or the mind to comprehend.

Remember Walter Benjamin's statement that,

> The apparatus that mediates the performance of the screen actor to the audience is not obliged to respect the performance as an entity. Guided by its operator, the camera comments on the performance continuously… the cinema audience is being asked to examine and report without any personal contact with the performer intruding.[241]

---

[239] Dyrness, *Visual*, 20.
[240] Ibid., 100.
[241] Benjamin, *Work*, 17-18.

In other words, the viewer passively receives what the camera shows us, interpreted by the film-maker, performers, sound engineers, lighting crew and all the other people involved in its creation. This, then, is not dissimilar to the processes of musical reproduction and carries with it the same issues of homogenization and creative lack.

In the use of ready-made video, we are not thinking original thoughts, developing original theology informed by Scripture, reason, tradition and experience, we are merely recycling thoughts already presented. We are not being creative in our use of visual media and the cinematographic since the creative aspects of it have already been completed. We are merely witnesses to an already complete creativity, and we become observers of thoughts and interpretations that have already taken place in the mind of the creator. The same could be said of photography, in which the interpretation is performed by the creator of the image, as opposed to a painting where the representation is made but the interpretation is left open to the viewer. 'Paintings are made with time and difficulty, material complexity, textural depth, talent and craft, imagination and "mindfulness". A good painting is a rich and vigorous thing. A photograph, however well lit, however cleverly set up, only has one layer of content. It is all there on the surface. You see it, you've got it.'[242]

As Kimball states, 'A church may use multisensory worship and expensive video projectors to connect to the culture and communicate about Jesus and Kingdom living. If it ends there, however, it becomes sin. It becomes narcissistic. It creates another generation of Christian consumers who consume the worship experience their

---

[242] Jones, 'Flat'.

church provides.'[243] Herein lies the problem with some use of screens and image in some churches - it seems to create an apparent alliance to manufactured entertainment rather than to transcendence. In endeavouring to make themselves part of the world, most churches have lost the sense that they should be apart from it - enabling people to find solace and rest from the hectic, ever-changing pace of everyday life. In providing a deep, sustained encounter with God through aesthetic experience, churches can provide a stability and solidity that most people crave.

David Peterson makes an excellent summary of the discussion when he says,

> We could... consider the effect of other electronic media on what we do together. For example, when we address God by reading words together from a screen, does it change the character of prayer? What is the impact of using video clips, visual art or music in a sermon? What is the value of having someone address a congregation through a video link?... Preachers and service leaders need to reckon with ministry in a media-saturated society and to be discerning about the positive and negative implications for their gatherings.[244]

The danger with rejecting outright the visual culture of which we are a part, is that in doing so we reject an important means of reaching the unreached, a means of communicating with *visual* Christians, and we reject an important outlet for the creativity of those who have the talent and ability to create video and photography that expresses worship within the local context and edifies both them and their congregation. Peterson's key word here is 'discernment.'

---

[243] Kimball, *Emerging*, 227.
[244] Peterson, *Encountering*, 81.

Some churches have even gone so far as to embrace social media within their gathering, reasoning that we must be all things to all people in order that we may win some (1Cor 9:22).[245] For churches to have a social media presence in the 21st century is probably essential given its importance in contemporary society[246] and as a platform for evangelism to what Leonard Sweet terms 'digital natives.'[247]

But while social media in the context of evangelism is one thing (and it is true that some social media can provide a useful platform for making contact with people and for debating topical issues from a Christian perspective) a relationship that is based solely on that superficial contact, and which never progresses beyond it, is unhealthy and to the ultimate detriment of the church. It must be considered then, that the use of sites such as Twitter and Facebook within the corporate gathering contributes little to a sense of engagement with God or with the people in the congregation. As Archbishop of Canterbury, Justin Welby remarks, 'Instant reaction has replaced reflective comment… The best answer to a complex issue… is not always given in 140 characters.'[248] Sometimes the world of social media makes it easier to engage with people thousands of miles away than with the people in our immediate vicinity.

However, given the social significance of the Internet and social media today, it is of vital importance that churches consider carefully how they will use it and what they stand

---

[245] This is the basis of Ed Stetzer's argument in *Christianity Today,* Feb 2015.

[246] Some interesting statistics can be found at www.pewinternet.org which states that 71% of American online adults were regular Facebook users in 2014.

[247] Sweet, *Carpe Mañana.*

[248] Welby as quoted by Bingham, 'Reflection'.

to gain and lose by its use. How does social media change the nature of relationships? What does it say about a church that values the use of social media over face-to-face conversation? Is it even necessary to use social media to engage with the community around us when many people seem to be crying out for physical interaction? 'Churches have begun to use blogs, chat areas, and electronic bulletin boards in their efforts to build community. Yet there remains the danger of people finding connection through these electronic forms and believing they have found genuine intimacy. This can cause them to miss out on authentic community with the people they worship with each week.'[249] Social media has a tendency towards distraction, and if we wish to consider worship as something deep and sustained, then it most certainly can have no place within our corporate expression.

Drane observes that, 'Many of the Church's problems over how to contextualize worship in this new situation arise from the way in which we have allowed literate culture to be absolutised as if it was the only way of doing things.'[250] and so we must also consider that a return to some pre-technological *good old days* is not a solution. We are a part of a technological culture and we must engage with it. The danger comes in allowing the culture to dictate how that engagement takes place. 'A preacher who confines himself to considering how a medium can increase his audience will miss the significant question: In what sense do new media alter what is meant by religion, by church, even by God?'[251]

At the most basic level, even our liturgical forms might be considered a technology, since they are a system that shapes what we do and say in our corporate worship

[249] Hipps, *Culture*, 112.
[250] Drane, *McDonaldization*, 165.
[251] Postman, *Technopoly*, 19.

expression. Certain forms of liturgy like the Anglican Church's *Common Worship*, use formal language and structures that might tend a musical director to choose more formal music - hymns and anthems. A liturgical structure that is less formalized (and some might suggest less artificial) creates a more relaxed and open approach to music. Those at the *hymn* end of the worship wars suggest that such informality breeds flippancy and a lack of respect towards a great, awesome and utterly transcendent God. Those at the *pop song* end of the spectrum suggest that such formality leads to coldness, distance and lack of emotion in corporate worship, causing people to forget the immanence of God through the indwelling of the Holy Spirit and the incarnation of Christ. In either case, the way we approach God, and the behaviour we manifest is shaped by the pattern, by the system, by the *technology* of our liturgy.

Being conscious of all the devices and systems we use - from the liturgy to social media, from the instruments we use to the way we organize our seating - and being discerning in their use within corporate worship, and how they affect the expression of our relationship with God and each other, then, is incredibly important.

Worship, Creativity & the Spiritual

So what represents true creativity in worship? We have already defined creativity to be, in its deepest sense, an expression of our humanity, reflecting the creative nature of God himself. Therefore, we must consider that, for our worship to be truly creative, it must express our humanity not just as it relates to God but also in our relationship to each other.

'God is spirit, and his worshippers must worship in spirit and in truth.' (John 4:24). Our corporate worship, then, must connect God's spirit and ours, in an identity of understanding, thought and action, that our will and God's become aligned, the logical outcome of our transformation into the likeness of Christ (Rom 12:1-2). It must also be worship in truth - which indicates the role of the intellect in worship. This is not emotionalism or sentimentality, but a deep connection to the transcendent, Almighty God, made known through Jesus and present in each believer by the indwelling of the Holy Spirit. Peterson suggests that many churches use John 4:24 as an argument for the use of spiritual gifts, or for an over-prescriptive approach to corporate worship. He proposes that this verse is better suited to an understanding of worship as an 'engagement with God that he has made possible through the revelation of himself in Jesus Christ and the life he has made available through the Holy Spirit.'[252]

At the heart of truly *spiritual* worship lies an understanding that our corporate gatherings are to be a deep and 'sustained encounter'[253] with God which is ultimately transformative. 'People grow in conformity to what they love. The worship of God tends to transform the worshiper into the likeness of God.'[254] Therefore, a limited understanding of worship, which reduces it to a few songs on a Sunday morning and does not endeavour to introduce more of the artful into our corporate expression will grow stunted and unbalanced disciples - whole congregations will be nothing but mouths, since so much of what we do is verbal - rather than properly developed bodies, metaphorically, incorporating all the senses (1Cor 12).

Perhaps, then, musicians need to be prepared to sacrifice some of their current pre-eminence in corporate worship in order to make room for other forms of expression.

---

[252] Peterson, *Engaging*, 100.

[253] Cherry, *Architect*, 17.

[254] Phenix, *Education*, 165.

Could it be that music shouldn't be so dominant in our Sunday services? And in making it so, are we just reflecting our culture rather than transforming it? Maybe we should consider the specialness of music as an art form, and the saturation levels it has reached within our everyday lives, and reduce the amount we use in our services so that we can restore the sense of its specialness, and consequently genuinely *listen* to the music that we encounter rather than it being a mere background hum to our lives, restoring listening as a conscious experience rather than an ambient one. In contrast to the relentless noise of music and speech both in and out of church, perhaps congregations, too, would do well to re-learn the purpose of silence. A deep, sustained and transformative encounter is also one that provides time for introspection and thought. This would seem to be antithetical to the technological world.

If we are to make space for silence, and for deeper exploration and contemplation then we must also consider the place of the clock within our worship. Some services begin with a countdown to the start of the service and then time everything to the minute so that the service concludes at precisely the time they have set. This is programmatic worship at its most extreme.[255] The problem is that time demands to be filled.[256] This, then, is what determines the lack of silence within church. Time is activity opposed to stillness. 'From our division of time into uniform, visualisable units,' McLuhan says, 'comes our sense of duration and our impatience when we cannot endure the delay between events.'[257] Efficiency may be suitable for a concert performance, but it is most certainly

---

[255] Note that I do not say 'contemporary' in form. There are some churches that worship in a formal, traditional style who can be just as prescriptive.
[256] Which bears comparison with Parkinson's Law.
[257] McLuhan, *Understanding*, 157.

not suited to a deep and sustained encounter with God, or to the building of significant relationships within the Christian community. We end up with the show of faith, but none of its substance.

Efficiency is one of the key identifiers of McDonaldization, but in the context of worship it is, as Marva Dawn says, 'extremely destructive of true worship in multiple ways.'[258] Along with the stifling of free expressions of praise, and shortened sermons, curtailed prayers and community concerns, she considers worst that 'there is no time for silence and the surprising workings of the Holy Spirit.'[259]

> Christians mimic the frantic lifestyle of the world around them and have no understanding that God has designed a wonderful rhythm of rest and work, of refreshment and then response. In that rhythm, we don't have to rush out of the worship service at precisely noon, since there is no work to do on a Sunday. The day is set apart for worship, for relationships, for growing in our sense of who God is and who we are as individuals desiring to become like Jesus and as a community of his people displaying his character to the world.[260]

Worship, Creativity & the Relational

Since Peterson suggests a definition of worship that extends beyond music to a wider concept of a sustained encounter with God that leads to our transformation as individuals and as a whole church body, it must be considered that true, creative worship will have a profound impact on our relationships. In what ways, then, can worship be considered relational?

---

258 Dawn, *Reaching*, 42.
259 Ibid.
260 Ibid., 43.

Constance Cherry invites us to consider the word 'corporate' - which derives from the Latin for 'body' - *corpus*. 'Thus an experience is corporate,' she says, 'if it is a matter of belonging to or being united in one body.'[261] But the devices and systems that we use within contemporary corporate worship, as we have discussed, have a tendency towards individualization. As Cherry points out, 'corporate worship is not what takes place at a given church simply because an aggregate group of individual worshippers show up at the announced time of service. Rather, corporate worship is what happens when the body of Christ assembles to hear with one heart and speak with one voice the words, phrases, prayers, petitions, and thanks fitting to Christian worship.'[262] The reason we sing as a church is not to feel good within ourselves, or even as an artistic expression, but it is the fact that we sing *together* that binds us as a body, the power of voices united in the praise of their Creator that builds us up as a body of believers. So what good is corporate singing if the musical style hinders rather than helps it - be it the volume of the instrumentation, an unpredictable melody, or one that requires such a large vocal range that it is too high for some and too low for others.[263]

In opting for a form of corporate worship that seeks to replicate the rock concert, or the Christian conference - the church misses the wider point of meeting together. 'The church is about the big weekend encounter, but once the people have had their encounters, everyone goes their separate ways. The worship experience has little to do with sharing life together and nothing to do with corporate mission in the world. It is about personal transformation and private faith.'[264]

---

[261] Cherry, *Architect*, 12.
[262] Ibid., 13.
[263] There are both hymns and modern songs that are guilty of these.
[264] Hipps, *Hidden*, 150.

Writing for the magazine *On Religion,* 25-year old Andrew Grey dismisses the approach many churches have towards technology in their attempts to attract a younger age group through the doors, 'These gestures are largely unsuccessful because they are often inauthentic.' he says, 'Rather than trying its best to mimic young people's transient fashions and trends, it should be offering the message that young people - indeed all people - desperately need to hear: you are accepted. More than accepted - you are loved.'[265]

Churches are not failing because they adopt or do not adopt technology in worship, they are not failing because of cultural relevance or irrelevance (and if postmodernism truly exists, there is no such thing). Churches are failing because the message of community, the message of unity and togetherness goes against the prevailing culture. You can have all the flashing lights and videos you want, but it will not change the fact that society has decided that church no longer represents what most people believe about society, about themselves and about community. The church's story is no longer their story. What changes, then? Do we change to fit in with a culture that sees people become more and more isolated and individualized? Or do we seek to take a better message out, to demonstrate love and community among believers and invite those struggling with modern existence to become part of something greater? What world should we show a new or non-Christian when they eventually step through the doors of the church? A service that mimics the frantic and frenetic pace of the outside world? Or something that is founded on stability, on peace and on deep relationships with others and with God?[266]

---

[265] Grey, 'Attract'.

[266] Once again, weak relationships are a problem common to both 'traditional' and 'contemporary' church, largely owing to our sense that 'worship' is something that only takes place between 10 and 11am (or whenever) on a Sunday morning. The tyranny of the clock is not

'A congregation so concerned not to cause offense that it manages to entertain and amuse but never to *worship God* either in the way it lives or in its corporate life carries little credibility to a burned-out postmodern generation that rejects linear thought yet hungers for integrity of relationships.'[267]

Worship, Creativity & Contextualization

Connected to the relational issues of increasingly technologically dependent forms of corporate worship are issues of contextualization, also linked with the homogenization of contemporary worship music. 'Worship, of all aspects of church life, ought to create a context in which people can be themselves, which is another way of saying that we need spaces where we may celebrate the way God has made us.'[268]

However, our technological choices have led to the homogenization of the church at the expense of cultural diversity. Even in churches where different nationalities gather for worship, to express unity in Christ in spite of diversity of culture, the musical worship is invariably Western in form. Neither is the idea that contemporary Christian music is somehow the 'one best way' to express worship confined to large churches. Smaller congregations take their lead from the marketplace and the conference as well. Rather than seeking to find ways of worshiping together that express their common identity, they all too readily opt for the quick-fix technological solution. Products like Musicademy's backing track software[269] only serve to emphasize an expectation of music that must be

---

conducive to the development of anything other than superficial relationships.

[267] Carson, 'Word,' 60.
[268] Drane, *McDonaldization*, 170.
[269] www.musicademy.com/worship-backing-band.

performed in a particular way, by particular instruments to a particular standard. Churches are led to believe that they cannot worship without a five-piece worship band. Rather than seeking local solutions, raising up and investing in talented individuals within the congregation, which creates a worship form that is contextual, relational and spiritually enriching, leadership is given the easy option of bypassing individual and corporate development altogether. Solutions like this only serve to encourage the status quo.

Locally appropriate answers to questions of worship form should first take into account engagement with God in a deep, sustained manner and the way it is expressed in fellowship with other believers - that is, how it works out in development of relationships and in mutual edification. None of these priorities even suggest that music should be the first and foremost way in which this dynamic is expressed. Small congregations, lured into the notion that worship consists of music performed by a large band should instead consider that worship in Scripture is frequently expressed in a non-musical fashion. If music's primary function within the context of the corporate gathering is one of edification for believers and a response to a daily revelation of God's work in their everyday lives, then congregations without musical resources can easily consider other ways in which they can encourage each other and express gratitude to God, perhaps through greater use of the poetic, spoken word, dance, dramatic or visual artforms. The technological solution serves only to lure us into the notion that music (and a particular genre of music at that) is the 'one best way' of worshiping.

If we are locked into Western forms of worship music, this can also serve to exclude those from a non-Western background who may be part of our gathering. In singing exclusively Western songs, we fail to value cultures other than our own. If we are to be truly creative in worship, we must find ways of being inclusive - either by creating non-musical means of worship that can include everyone, or by writing or performing songs that permit both Western and non-Western cultures to participate together.

This idea of contextualization should not only be considered from a multicultural point of view, but also multi-generationally. Here, the same principles of inclusiveness apply. Musicians must be prepared to subsume their own tastes and musical preferences for the sake of the members of the congregation, finding ways in which all can take part and express their relationship with God and with each other.

The separation of different age groups and nationalities into exclusive congregations each worshiping in their own form is not the solution. Consider this from a multi-generational point of view. In separating the old from the young, the young miss out on the richness of tradition and the depth of knowledge and experience that an older generation brings, while conversely, the older generation misses out on the energy, vitality and desire to grow exhibited by the young. Each generation learns, feeds and grows from the other, creating disciples of rounded character and theological depth. Likewise, in becoming separated along national lines, believers of all ages miss out on the insights of people who view the world and faith in a way that is different and fresh, that challenges our own preconceptions and can open our hearts and minds to mission in other parts of the world. In the UK's increasingly multicultural society - not to mention with a demographic that is getting steadily older - these are issues that must be addressed urgently by many churches.

Conclusion

Truly creative worship is spiritual, relational and contextual, a state of being and not just an activity. It values the edification of the gathered church and sets aside its own preferences for the preferences of others. It values performance as a means of artistic expression reflecting the creative nature of God in humankind. It seeks to find ways to express love of God and love of neighbour both in everyday activity and in the context of the congregation. 'Praise provides Christians with the opportunity to confess together what they believe about God. So it becomes a way of realigning ourselves with his character and will. Praise edifies the church and encourages faithfulness to God in everyday living.'[270] These ways are both musical and non-musical.

Is technology utterly opposed to these things? Is it the antithesis of creative worship? Not entirely, but it does tend to prize the mechanical over the human, the quick-fix over the mess of working together, speed over craftsmanship, the economic over the human, the quantifiable over the qualitative. It can be inhuman, soulless and anaesthetic. It is of these negative tendencies that we must be conscious when we employ technology within corporate worship, and the arguments for technology - that see it as necessary for a younger generation to express themselves - are not entirely true, as we have seen. So we must be careful in doing so that we do not get caught up in a 'cult of youth' that sees everything new and shiny as good and casts out tradition and depth that has been crafted and refined over centuries.

---

[270] Peterson, *Encountering*, 126.

'If faith is to communicate it must be expressed in culture. Culture, however, is never neutral.'[271] The commodification and homogenization of worship music as a reflection of wider contemporary culture is a danger to healthy and proper expression of worship within the church. 'It is easy to get caught up in the exciting and ever changing culture of worship events, new songs and CD releases and fail to be critical or analytical in the way we use these new forms of expression.'[272]

This is entering a world of marketing gimmickry that has little to do with the deeper purpose of church. However, '[The danger is] of sidelining, stifling what Christians will want to describe as a God-given calling to develop fresh forms of order in a modern/postmodern culture that is riven with powerful forces of repetition, replication and homogenization.'[273] So we are driven to the conclusion that, like it or not, we are part of the modern, technological world. Even so, technophobia is not the solution. It is far more constructive to consider issues of *need* within corporate worship. What is necessary to worship? Do we really *need* microphones, drums, screens, lighting and smoke machines in order to worship? Is it appropriate to our local context? Does it build relationship and spiritual integrity or does it hinder growth through an over-reliance on the idea that we must *feel* in order to worship?

To what extent must we be part of contemporary culture in order to reach it? As White asks, 'to what extent should Christian worship be created and understood as a countercultural force, an activity that calls into question the values and presuppositions of the age of technology, and to what extent it should conform to the kinds of

---

[271] Ward, *Selling*, 165.
[272] Ibid., 166.
[273] Begbie, *Resounding*, 255-6.

contemporary expectations that the prevalence of technology has fostered?'[274]

This question lies at the heart of the issue of the extent to which technology is stifling creativity within corporate worship. Contemporary church is becoming more and more mediated. We need to recover the contextual, relational and spiritual elements of our corporate worship and reconnect with the past. We should not sacrifice our creativity and emotion for cold logic and efficiency, but neither must we sacrifice theological truth for purely artistic license. 'God's people must [reread]...the biblical text in the reality of the lived world rather than in the safety of old assumptions.'[275] A balance must be struck.

---

[274] White, *Worship*, 120.
[275] Detweiler, *Matrix*, 152.

4

REBALANCING TECHNOLOGY IN CORPORATE WORSHIP

The mediator between head and hands must be the heart!
– Fritz Lang's *Metropolis*

We began our exploration of the place of technology in corporate worship with the idea that many churches feel it a necessity to import programmatic forms of worship into a context for which they may be entirely inappropriate. At the heart of the decision to create a model of corporate worship based on a conference or on the prevailing trend in the Christian worship music industry, is an assumption that the quantity of people attending any given service is the means by which that church or service is deemed *successful*.

In accepting this as a model for church, we become part of an industrialized worldview that is more common to the supermarket or the shopping mall than it is for disciples of Christ. It considers quality of faith as measurable by the numbers of people that come through the door, or by the numbers of activities that a church undertakes and it considers that in order to reach out to the postmodern world it must, to a certain extent, *mimic* the postmodern world. In order to accomplish what it perceives as its mission, this type of church employs more and more technology in order to make it accessible to modern (or postmodern) Christians and non-Christians alike.

The introduction to this book, then, presented a dilemma. We posited two fictional churches - one entirely technological, the other struggling to keep up with the demands of contemporary society. To compete and survive, the struggling church adopted the forms of the first without any consideration as to the impact that this might have. Even though it worked in terms of attracting more numbers through the doors, there was a sense that the church may have lost something in the process.

To decide whether this was, in fact, the case, we needed to define what we meant by the word *technology*. This proved to be slightly more complicated than suggesting that technology was simply the gadgets that are so prevalent in our digital society. Technology in general, and in music in particular, concerns almost all of how we interact with the world around, and of how we create, perform and listen to music. Technology, it was concluded, is not just the devices we use, but the systems within which we use them. Key to this are two theories which describe this interaction.

The first of these comes from Marshall McLuhan: 'the medium is the message'.[276] This suggests that technological devices and systems influence the nature and scope of normal human activity. As he puts it, 'the medium... shapes and controls the scale and form of human

---

[276] McLuhan, *Understanding*, 7.

association and action.'[277] And that 'Physiologically, man *in the normal use of technology…* is perpetually modified by it and in turn finds ever new ways of modifying his technology [italics mine].'[278] To him, even language itself is a technology, being as it is a system of communication, 'Words are complex systems of metaphors and symbols that translate experience into our uttered… senses. They are a technology of explicitness.'[279] This raises an interesting question - if words and writing translate our experience into something that can be apprehended by another through sense perception, may we describe music similarly? Does music allow us to express things that cannot be expressed any other way? Is music a metaphor for unutterable experience?

What is key here is our attempt to avoid the idea that the technology we use is in any way neutral, be it a physical device (hard technology) or an operating system (soft technology). Technologies influence the way we live, our worldview and, from the Christian standpoint, our theology. Technology is 'value-laden', to use Stephen Monsma's terminology.[280]

The second major theory that endeavours to come to grips with our technological society is George Ritzer's *McDonaldization* thesis. He proposes the existence of a force exerted on society by the idea that there is a 'one-best way' of performing any task. This idea he calls McDonaldization which he divides into four categories: efficiency, calculability, predictability and control. McDonaldization is essentially a process-driven way of performing tasks that leads to a specified and repeatable outcome. The epitome of this is, of course, the

---

[277] McLuhan, *Understanding*, 9.

[278] Ibid., 51.

[279] Ibid., 63.

[280] Monsma, *Responsible*.

McDonald's chain of restaurants, although it can equally apply to companies such as IKEA or Starbucks. In this kind of organization, efficiency ensures that the product is made for the cheapest price in the quickest manner; calculability that each part of the process is measurable and can be altered to ensure maximum efficiency (the 'one best way'); predictability means that the customer knows what to expect which gives a high degree of assurance of a certain level of quality; finally, control, is tied into predictability in that it creates a standardized environment allowing for greater calculability and efficiency.

These two theories taken together allowed us to expand our definition of technology beyond that of specific devices, which would otherwise lead to unnecessary and unproductive arguments, into a world of effects. It allowed us to define technology not by pointing to a physical object, or even to a particular process, but by noting effects - in the same way that we might define *wind* by seeing it move the trees.

The first effect concerns the way we view *time*. Lewis Mumford famously described the clock as the key machine of the modern age,[281] and through our examination it is easy to see how he reaches this conclusion. Tying into McDonaldization's notion of ultimate efficiency, the clock becomes a tyrant demanding that we compartmentalize our lives into work and *not-work*. Our lives become increasingly regulated because it is necessary for the economic well-being of the country that we produce a certain amount, or in a service economy, that we *process* a certain amount of people or achieve whatever designated, measurable outcomes we have been assigned. Since time and efficiency are measurable quantities there is status (and money) to be gained through busyness, even though our

---

[281] Mumford, *Technics*, 14.

technological devices have created a world where it is possible to work less. In being forced to operate at the speed of the machine and the microchip, our world has become one of instant reaction rather than considered response.

The second effect concerns *homogenization*, technology encourages standardization through rules, regulation and bureaucratic systems. It ties into the notion of predictability. Uniformity encourages a minimum standard and a predictable expectation. When we enter a McDonald's or buy a piece of furniture from IKEA, we know what we will get regardless of our geographical location. While this might be considered good in terms of quality control, it is often the case that when a uniform average is set, there is no scope or incentive for people to excel. Systems and procedures that create uniformity leads to the atrophying of human creativity and a lack of cultural diversity. It also leads to an increased risk-aversion and, because things like creativity are ultimately unquantifiable, we become hemmed in by systematization - ever more unable and incapable of doing anything truly new.

Our third effect concerns the concept of *progress*. The world is changing at an enormously rapid pace and we have very little time to assimilate the changes that are upon us even before we realize it.[282] Consider the case of Facebook. Launched in 2004, before its tenth anniversary it had nearly 1.3 billion users. As of January 2015, if it were a country, Facebook would be the most populous nation on earth.[283] It is visited by one third of the UK and US populations every day.[284] Almost within the space of a decade, we have become a world where social media

---

[282] Warman, 'Trends.'
[283] Stenovec, 'Facebook.'
[284] Sedghi, 'Facebook.'

127

dominates the everyday experience of most people on the planet.

This is not to mention some of the more subtle and small scale changes that we encounter on a regular basis. We are not yet in a position to assess the impact of ever increasing processor and internet speeds, or to question the growth in the robotics industry, or in the surveillance society, or the introduction of the driverless car, or the impact of music streaming websites on the creation and performance of music. To an extent we are still assimilating the impact of the TV in a world where 71 percent of Britons say they are 'always looking at screens.'[285] It is well-documented that our use of mobile phones is having an impact on our ability to sleep, and that our attention spans, imaginations and ability to process complex thought are suffering as a consequence of our viewing habits.

Coupled with this is the idea of *novelty*. In an ever-changing society, it is perhaps unsurprising that we are gripped by the desire for all things new. In doing so, we create a *cult of youth* that values the abilities of the young and their facility with technology while apparently discarding the skills and traditions of the old as obsolete and worthless. And an endless procession of *upgrades* leads to a confusion of *need* with *desire*. Christina Crook suggests that, 'If people of character are formed by attachment, local cultures and local responsibilities... our "up-at-all-costs" mentality may be the wrong target.' She suggests that the physical act of making is 'personal and powerful more than ever in a throwaway culture... Our technological advancements,' she states, 'have one trajectory: *up*. Up the corporate ladder, *up* in social status, *up* and away from our

---

surroundings, our physical demands, from the bore of the everyday.'[286]

In seeking to discover the positives of these aspects of technology, and to the processes characterizing McDonaldization, it appears that while there are indeed some things to be gained from engagement with the world of efficiency, calculability, predictability and control, it seems that the McDonaldized world exists in an ultra-sensitive balance that only takes the slightest of nudges to tip it into the negative. If, then, this is the world with which we are to engage as Christians, and particularly within our corporate worship, we must be extremely conscious of this balancing act.

Summary: Technology & Music

It follows, then, that our technology is going to have an equally profound impact on our art and music. This we considered in the second chapter. Initially, recordings of music were made in order to preserve certain live performances. However, once music was made into something tangible and marketable, it became subject to 'technological determinism'[287] and the traits of McDonaldization. This becomes evident when we look at way the recording processes work to remove music from its immediate context and create something permanent out of an essentially transitory art form.

Once something is made into a physical object, it has the potential to become a product, and in becoming

---

[286] Crook, 'Joy.'

[287] See Katz, *Capturing*, 3. Technological determinism is the idea that tools, machines and other artefacts of human invention have unavoidable, irresistible consequences for users and for society in general. This bears considerable similarity to McLuhan's 'medium is the message' thesis.

commodified, the culture of music is changed. Live performance becomes technologically mediated in that it must match the recording. Playing styles change, interpretations become attempts to replicate rather than to create. Music's success is not gauged by any artistic measure but on quantifiable sales. In creating more and more recordings, music becomes ubiquitous in society and is no longer listened to but becomes the soundtrack to everyday life.

In order to ensure greater sales, musicians and recording companies seek a popular and simple formula. This is then coupled with a marketable image which is then spread across the globe via TV, Radio and the Internet. In this way, music becomes increasingly homogenized. The diet of popular music to which the majority of us are subject on a daily basis either by the office radio or on the factory floor, is not music to be listened to and thoughtfully considered. This is music that is played *at* you rather than *to* you. It is music simply designed to cover the silence or to increase productivity. The problem is that the more we are exposed to this background music, the less able we are to accept anything more refined. This is known as *regressive listening*.[288]

This commodified and homogenized music is invariably designed as a *mood modifier*. Rather than seeking to engage deep emotion, if it evokes anything, it is superficial sentimentality. This music is not the 'tonal analogue to life'[289] but semi-therapeutic catharsis, designed to do little more than to distract us from the realities of modern living.

---

[288] Adorno, 'Fetish,' 51.
[289] Langer, *Feeling*, 27.

This led us to examine what we actually mean by the term *creativity* and how it relates to technology. In doing so, we discovered that music itself is inherently technological, in that it operates within structures and systems, but also that it can remain creative as well as commercial, as in the case of great composers like Bach or Mozart. True human creativity draws on a depth of tradition and something that we might term *spirituality*. Since the issue, then, becomes one of extent, a whole slew of questions arise. To what extent is our music mediated by technology? What is valued in our music? Is it quality over quantity? Commercial success over tradition and human expressiveness? Humanity over the mechanical? Craftsmanship over mass-production?

Depending on our answers to these kinds of questions, we are led to conclude that music points us to our whole human nature as intellectual, emotional and spiritual beings, or else it reminds us of the imperfections of our nature - and calls us to be better than we are.

Summary: Technology, Music & the Church

The third chapter brought the discussion closer to home as we considered how all the different aspects of McDonaldization and modern musical culture have infiltrated our church life, often unconsciously. We noted how the word *worship* has become entirely associated with music, despite the fact that this definition has little basis in Scripture. We also saw that in many cases, *worshiping* was equated with a type of emotional rush, rather than one rooted in a response of love and service to a revelation of the nature of God. We saw how many churches, in seeking this *worship experience* base their services around conference models that are inappropriate for the local context and that, as *worship* and *encounter with God* are experienced through music, many churches, particularly those involved in the organization of these conferences, produce albums under the guise of *resources*, to help mediate the worship experience. The most successful of these are produced by major labels like EMI who, as with cinema, see the Christian as just another marketing sector. Worship music loses any sense of the sacred and becomes classified alongside rock, pop and classical as just another genre - or indeed sub-genre. As a consequence, it, too, has its quality measured in terms of sales and popularity.

As it becomes commodified, *worship music* becomes increasingly homogenized, for exactly the same reasons as any other genre of music. This, in turn, leads to churches requiring increasing amounts of electronics to recreate the sounds of the recording, or the atmosphere of the conference, regardless of whether it is contextually appropriate. Meanwhile, the production of albums leads us to approach worship music in the same way as we would approach any other form of music and brings us to the same dangers of mood modification and regression of listening.

In addition, the technological church, in seeking to be relevant to contemporary culture, takes in other systems and devices, without thought for how they might affect our relationships with each other, with the community around or with God himself. Architectural and liturgical changes are made to accommodate devices and systems that may be, once again, entirely inappropriate to the local context. A lack of thought and consideration turns church from an active demonstration of loving community to a passive concert programme. True worship responds to God's revelation of himself in a manner that is based on a deep understanding of his nature, that expresses itself in love to others, and that in expressing this love is appropriate to the local context, permitting engagement for people from every culture and background.

Four Approaches To Technology

It is possible to describe four different ways in which churches interact, consciously or unconsciously, with technology and technological culture. In examining the pros and cons of each in turn, we should come to a better understanding of our own attitudes, and what, if anything, can be done to mitigate the negative impact of contemporary culture on our spiritual life. To a certain extent, these four approaches represent distinct extremes. Most churches are likely to contain different aspects of each approach within their congregation.

1.   Techno-apathy

This, one suspects, is the most common stance for many churches today. Techno-apathy betrays a lack of care and consciousness of what defines technology and both the positive and negative impact it may have on corporate worship. Put simply, techno-apathy is a view that neither knows nor cares. It shrugs its metaphorical shoulders and says that 'this is the way we have always done it.' It moves with the times as best it can according to the demographic of the congregation and the community within which it operates, endeavouring always to be relevant to contemporary society, but careless that an open door can let things in as well as out.

Even an approach like this can have its positive aspects, however. In accepting the status quo, it avoids conflict - the congregation are unified in their acceptance of things as they are. This being so, the approach pleases most of them. They are happy enough to turn up for their Sunday service and accept dutifully, if perhaps a little joylessly, what is placed in front of them. Such a corporate gathering will accept the musical style of the majority culture within the church. Any minority groups within the congregation will accept this as the way things are and make no effort to change them. Techno-apathy will constitute a blend of the traditional and the modern, digital and analogue simply by virtue of inactivity. They will sing the popular hymns of bygone days - possibly accompanied by an organ, or synthesized equivalent. They will also accept more contemporary forms, possibly led by a small band. The two musical groups (organist and band) will remain separate within the service, however. They may even regard each other with a degree of suspicion. This is a church that is carried along by culture, and to that extent is relevant to it. Even as they ignore the trends of contemporary church, they will nevertheless choose music on the basis of popularity - the most common reason for choosing a particular song will be that 'it's one of my favourites.'

From the negative viewpoint, this approach is passive and uncritical. There is little in the way of theological scrutiny of their worship structures or musical forms. Such a church may seek to engage with the community, but finds itself at a loss to understand the post-modern, post-Christian world. It has not considered things like the pace of change in the world and how it affects individuals in their employment. They may have an online presence in the form of a website or social media page, but it will only be maintained in the most half-hearted fashion. They do it because it is 'the done thing nowadays', but they don't really understand why, or put much effort into managing it. This is a purely reactive church - it is unengaged, uncreative and unimaginative.

In an increasingly technological world this is an untenable stance. As a church we cannot afford to ignore the world, or adopt what happens to be current without thought or careful consideration. Like it or not, we live in a technological world, and it is up to us to decide whether we will embrace it or reject it. But the apathetic church is one that is constantly clinging to the coat-tails of contemporary society. Detweiler and Taylor ask the question: 'Will religious and educational leaders play hardball with kids hooked on instant access? Or will we pump up the volume in our teaching and preaching as our culture seeks a quiet, humane alternative? We fear that people of faith used to playing constant catch-up will embrace technology at the very moment the dot-com generation rejects it.'[290]

2. Techno-sympathy

The techno-sympathetic, or the technophile, church is a happy adopter of all things technological. Although typified by organizations like Hillsong or Soul Survivor, it is by no means exclusive to this kind of setup. It is a church that loves all things new. It will follow the latest digital trends avidly and seek ways to apply them to their church setting. As a consequence of this, it could be seen to be a very mission-minded church, seeking to be immediately relevant and accessible to people, particularly teens and twenties, living in a world dominated by technology. By taking this approach, the church is contextual to much of Western culture, and is highly interactive with it. In being so, it is extremely able to understand and accept individuals, because it works within the technological structures of contemporary society and it is also very attractive to the digital natives it encounters as it represents something of the world they inhabit.

Within their expression of corporate worship, they see no problem with the use of video and computer graphics, nor with the use of smartphones, in the course of a service,[291]

---

[290] Detweiler & Taylor, *Matrix*, 40.
[291] Starner, 'Ways'.

no issue in employing contemporary music forms or in having a band controlled by the click of a metronome. This church will own the very latest in audio-visual equipment and where band members are absent they will turn to a technological solution in the form of pre-recorded backing tracks.[292] They will freely use and discard songs depending on their *effectiveness* in worship. Their musical preference, as befits their available instrumentation, and the demographic of the congregation, leans towards rock and pop styles.

The techno-sympathetic church suffers from the same issue of carelessness as a techno-apathetic church. It has uncritically adopted technology in order to appear *relevant* to the non-Christian culture and to an extent they are correct to do so, since there is no doubt that they have been hugely successful in bringing a new generation into church. It maintains high-quality production values, is professional, fast-moving, exciting and loud. In certain respects it is a highly missional stance - helping to present Christ and Christianity in familiar ways, seeking to turn otherwise secular form and values into something that aims to glorify Jesus.[293] Pop culture and the technological forms associated with it are valuable in making contact with a world that no longer reads books but prefers to watch television and surf the internet. Dyrness is cautious of this emphasis, however: 'Christians should not play the visual against the verbal. For Christians, who are people of the Book, the verbal revelation of God's Word will always have unique authority.'[294]

This kind of church, while appealing to a younger generation (although that in itself is debatable) will terrify the older. Yet the older, in an attempt to combat ageing

---

[292] Tyndale, 'Technology'.
[293] Neibuhr, *Christ*, 106.
[294] Dyrness, *Visual*, 156.

and dwindling congregations, will often turn to this type of model to attract younger people into church. This type of change, however, often takes place at the expense of established members who are driven away to churches providing more familiar and comfortable forms.

In creating performance/rock concert style services and in driving away an older generation, they lose touch with a sense of depth and tradition that has formed the church over hundreds of years. There is no sense of Christianity as a counter-cultural force, and the ritual of church becomes mechanistic, mindless, unimaginative and uncreative. 'If the church offers only the same things as the rationalized world of work, why should people who are oppressed elsewhere in their lives expect to find a resolution by joining the church?'[295]

Such services, however lively, are essentially unengaging, covering boredom and passivity with the noise of music and the flashing of lights. It is also, despite attracting large numbers, essentially unrelational since the experience is so individualistic. This is a reflection of the digital culture, '...The electronic age is essentially a tribe of individuals... We desire connection and community in our increasingly nomadic existence - yet we wander around the globe, glancing off other digital nomads without ever knowing or being known.'[296]

It is also non-contextual, as it considers that Western pop/rock forms will appeal to all members of the congregation. It will not seek in any way to incorporate the musical or artistic forms of other cultures as it pays no attention to any people group other than the English-speaking West. Because of this its corporate worship

---

[295] Drane, *McDonaldization*, 31.
[296] Hipps, *Pixels*, 107.

expression will be entirely mediated by screens and music. It may consider itself anti-liturgical, in the sense that there is little, if anything, in the way of formal prayers or litany and this contributes towards the overall passivity of the congregation. That being said, all the services performed will follow the same kind of structure which might be considered liturgical. The service is constructed in mechanical fashion, however - what Townley terms 'plug-and-chug'.[297]

3. Techno-antipathy

At the other end of the scale we find the techno-antipathetic, or technophobe, church. This kind of church is actively opposed to the use of the electronic devices that so dominate the life of the technophiles. But as we have already discussed, a completely non-technological stance is unrealistic since even liturgical forms might be seen as a technology, shaping our behaviour and the manner of our corporate worship. Their opposition is, therefore, based on a thoughtless, faulty definition of technology. Even to become as extreme in their anti-technological stance as to permit only unaccompanied singing is still not a complete rejection of technology since any musical system itself could be considered technological. Techno-antipathy, then, is more properly defined as a deep-rooted suspicion of electronic technology rather than as an outright rejection.

How does such a church approach its corporate worship then? On the positive side, it might be considered to be more relational and participative in that it involves more face-to-face interaction between people as well as perhaps having a more formal, liturgical style. Nevertheless, owing to this formality, such interaction is likely to be limited. A lack of electronics within the church does not necessarily

---

[297] Townley, *Designing*, 37.

mean that relationships will be any deeper, but simply that there is greater potential for depth given that there are fewer distractions. An anti-technological church finds its services mediated through people (i.e. its priests and other leaders) rather than through devices (i.e. screens, microphones, PA systems etc.). It is more likely that with such a formal setting, the congregation will be more conscious of the world around, and of the times and seasons that structure the life of the church.[298] This is something with which the darkened church of the technophile, lit entirely by artificial light, struggles to connect. Although it may be considered *analogue* in a digital world, this church preserves the traditions of the past, is aware of its heritage stretching from Scripture through to its historical place in the local community. This is a church with deep roots in a society that is rootless and shifting.

However, there are many negatives to such an approach. A church that is too rooted in the past has little concern for the present or the future. It sees changes in its local community and in wider culture and rejects them out of hand. In its suspicion and even active hatred of all things modern it loses the opportunity to connect with contemporary society. It is this stance that makes it a non-missional church - it exists in a cultural vacuum, unwilling or unable to relate to its immediate environment or the wider world. The knock-on effect of this is a church that is irrelevant, unimaginative and obsolete in the forms that it employs.

Apathy, Sympathy & Antipathy Analysed

There are plenty of churches that are sympathetic to technology that have deep relationships, are missional and

---

[298] The church year itself could be considered a technology as it a system that governs and influences the theology and overall life of the church as a whole.

outward focussed, that employ imaginative forms, that have congregations that are actively engaged and that place a value on their history and tradition while seeking to be *digital* in their outlook. Likewise there are plenty of antipathetic churches that are shallow in their relationships, that are so wedded to their forms and to their traditions that congregations are bored and unengaged, that are so *analogue* in their outlook that they have forgotten that the world outside has changed since Victorian times.

To suggest, then, that *technology*, as we have defined it, is the Pandora's box in which is contained all the troubles of the church, is over-simplistic and inaccurate. Leonard Sweet suggests that, 'The Old World Church refuses to change its culture to become more accessible. It either refuses to believe that anything much has changed in the culture or wants to live a separated lifestyle… The New World Church wants to live not a separated lifestyle from the world, but a sanctified lifestyle in the world. It is reverent about the message and agnostic about the medium.'[299]

While he is, to a certain extent, accurate, he misses the point. With the impact that technology and technological media have had on contemporary society, to be 'agnostic about the medium' is foolhardy. We have already seen from figures like McLuhan, Ritzer and Drane, that the devices and systems we employ influence our behaviour and worldview both in large and obvious ways but also in tremendously subtle and sometimes unforeseen ways. They affect our relationships, our ability to process ideas, and even the very nature of the ideas that we have in the first place.

---

[299] Sweet, *Pilgrims*, 141.

What tends to happen, however, is that the techno-antipathetic and techno-sympathetic stances become entangled in arguments regarding musical style, which as Dawn has said, is an unbiblical way of approaching worship.[300] So we must be careful we do not fall into that trap. Antipathy looks back and says that everything was better in the good old days. Sympathy looks to the present and the future and says that everything new is progress, despite the fact that this is patently not the case.[301] The one thing that characterizes each of the approaches is a measure of passivity, a general lack of care and thought when it comes to the nature and form of worship.

We must approach worship from the point of view of fostering community, preferring one another and seeking to be inclusive and to build each other up, expressing and practicing a transformation into the likeness of Christ (Rom 12:1-2). 'How many of the present conflicts over worship could be avoided if everyone remembered that the issue is not new forms for their own sake, but faithfulness to the gospel and true building up of the Christian community by contributions to people's growth in faith and knowledge and certainty!'[302]

One of the issues with a techno-sympathetic stance towards worship, according to most writers, is the tendency towards narcissism. Worship is shaped by the culture and so reflects the *me* centred nature of that culture. Worshippers become passive consumers, accepting the form and theology reflected therein in a

---

[300] Dawn, *Waste*, 187.
[301] Music produced by CD and internet streaming is a case in point. Despite making music more widely available than ever before, the compression of the sound produced by internet streaming is a reduction in quality compared with a CD, not an improvement. But the sympathetic person would still consider this progress.
[302] Dawn, *Waste*, 284.

passive and uncritical fashion. As we have seen throughout this book, technological devices play their part in emphasizing these aspects of human nature according to the principles laid down by McLuhan and Ritzer. 'It is not simply that most of us in the late-twentieth century rely heavily on technological ways and means of doing things in our daily life, but also that a technological worldview has pervaded society as a whole.'[303]

An outright rejection or technological antipathy, however, is not the answer. Our society, and our churches as part of that society, are inherently technological. People now relate to each other in ways that are almost entirely mediated by technology.[304] To suggest that we are even able to create a church that is entirely non-technological is an impossibility, since any music or liturgical form carries with it a technological influence. Is there a solution which does not confuse the issues of technology with issues of musical style, however closely related they may be? Is there a way to balance a suspicion of technology with its inevitability?

The Fourth Way: Techno-synthesis

The key aspects of any kind of techno-synthesis lie in an understanding of the nature of technology and the way in which it influences us - a clear, biblically-based theology of worship coupled with conscious thoughtfulness regarding the use of technology within the realm of corporate worship. Concerning the physical devices that we employ, we may also wish to include issues of ethics and social justice surrounding their manufacture.[305]

---

[303] White, *Change*, 14.

[304] Other than a direct face-to-face conversation, any other encounter with another human being is invariably technological in form.

[305] Monsma's book *Responsible Technology* is primarily concerned with this.

This is what the techno-synthesist seeks to do. Because they are conscious of the effects of technology on corporate worship, the synthesist approach is more relational than the others. It seeks to develop a quality of relationship over passive, performance models of worship. The approach is more critical and analytical of the content and context of worship, demonstrating awareness of individuals within the church and the place of the church within the wider community. In acknowledgement of a wide range of individuals within the congregation, not only will this approach seek to include other cultures where they are present, it will also seek to be multi-generational, blending both the old and the new, creating unity in diversity. This unity is not one that depends on a common musical taste or worship preference, but is based on inclusivity and relationship in Christ. In blending old and new, it also blends use and non-use of technological devices - the digital and the analogue.

It also accepts technology as a part of the modern world and the modern expression of church. It will reason that in order to reach out to a technological society, it must, to a certain extent, adopt some of the aspects of that society. However, it will also stand as a counter-cultural force, acknowledging that individuals need a place that is apart from the busyness and disorientation of everyday life. In particular, it may not pay such close attention to the clock, allowing the 'deep and sustained' encounter of which Constance Cherry speaks.[306] In this way, the synthesist church is a missional church, both multicultural and multi-generational in its worship, because its focus is on people rather than on programmes. It also acknowledges that 'Digital devices are great for sharing information, but not great for deepening human connections and a sense of belonging' and that we should use mobile devices 'to

---

[306] Cherry, *Architect*, 17.

augment, not to replace face-to-face interaction.'[307] In a society where, according to Susan Pinker, 'Britons of all ages now devote more time to digital devices and screens than to any other activity except sleeping,'[308] with the associated physical, mental (and one should add spiritual) health problems, the synthesist church is a church focussed on quality of relationships rather than on a quantitative *getting people through the doors*.

Finally, in its focus on quality, the corporate worship expression will always seek to be engaging and relevant to the people that form the congregation, recognizing the nature of their everyday lives, responding to events that affect the wider community, both joyful and sorrowful. The synthesist approach recognizes the culture of the time, but is not in thrall to it - either by wholesale adoption or by outright rejection. It is an approach that is not apathetic, but is active in its desire to understand and adapt culture to the purposes of engaging with God and with each other. Where the technophile and technophobe stances allow culture to define the agenda, a synthesist approach allows churches to make technology part of their culture on their terms. It ensures that technology is a servant rather than the master.

This is a fine line to walk and it must be said that it is easy for a church to begin to justify technological choices or anti-technological choices based on prejudice and stylistic preference. Where technological devices are permitted - most commonly through the use of the screen and musical amplification - it must be considered that these objects are not neutral tools, but carry with them an innate bias towards a particular form, an amplification of particular aspects of human nature as McLuhan has it.[309] Since the

---

[307] Pinker, 'Contact.'
[308] Ibid.
[309] McLuhan, *Understanding*, 7-23.

screen and modern forms of music can create a passive, concert programme performance atmosphere and outlook, ways to mitigate these effects must be considered carefully.

Rebalancing: Rediscovering Creativity

'While Christian worship may have the potential to transform the values of an age of technology, it has not often done so... In many cases, worship structures and processes have supported the status quo, rather than contributing to social change.'[310] To the extent that this is true, it is beholden to the church to rediscover something of the creativity that has made it the seat of cultural development throughout history.

We have already defined *creativity* as an expression of our being as made in the image of God and a reflection of our humanity in relationship both to God and to each other. This means that the technological world, which has a tendency to dehumanize and isolate,[311] stands, to a certain extent, as the antithesis of true creativity.

There is something significant in making music and other art *together*. There is a power in voices united in song - which is why the corporate song is something worth preserving in the face of performance models of worship. Indeed, our church worship is *corporate*. We express unity in community.

So how do we go about transforming the values of the age of technology? How do we break out of the homogenization, out of the sentimentalizing, the efficiency, calculability, the predictability and the control?

---

[310] White, *Change*, 125.

[311] From an artistic point of view, consider the bedroom pop star producing music without ever coming into physical contact with another human being.

How can we go about addressing the individualizing, dehumanizing, uncreative and programmatic aspects of technology that seem to have taken root within our corporate worship?

Let us return for a moment to our two churches. We saw an unsuccessful, dying village church adapt itself in order to draw people away from an apparently successful, modern church based in an industrial unit. The solution of the dying church was to endeavour to become like the modern one. Were they wrong to do so?

The answer, needless to say, is not a simple 'yes' or 'no'. The answer lies in the attitudes and outlook that frames their solution - which was purely a quantitative one dictated by a technological, McDonaldized world. They merely pulled people from one church to another - this is church in competition with itself, not seeking to be missional within its local context. This is a church that sees others as market rivals, not as fellow workers. Such a distorted viewpoint leads to an unconsidered, unthoughtful and unconscious adoption of technological forms. This has a profound impact beyond what is immediately obvious. As Scruton puts it, 'Changes in the liturgy are of great significance to the believer, since they are changes in the experience of God.'[312] He goes on to suggest that, in a world increasingly losing its sense of the sacred, we retain a deep desire for mystery. 'People experience a deep-down need for the thing that is not just desired but valued: the *unconsumable* thing, wanted not as a means but for its own sake, as an end.'[313]

The artist is in a position to mitigate the dehumanizing effects of technology in all its forms, to rediscover that

---

[312] Scruton, *Culture*, 19.
[313] Ibid., 33.

sense of the transcendent other, to realign the theology of the congregation to a bigger picture than is depicted by some of the more simplistic worship songs. 'Just because a song is sung over and over again doesn't mean that the singers are worshipping. Without something of substance in the song, without something for the mind to bite on, there can be no true worship. Without truth to feed on, worship will starve to death.'[314]

A thoughtfulness in the activity of the church brings with it a broader perspective of permitted art within the context of corporate worship. Creative corporate expression can take forms other than the musical and, indeed, it must if we are to avoid, once again, a distorted theology. Music is fit to emphasize some aspects of God, while other art forms, equally, express other facets of the Godhead. This permits us to see our faith expressed even in what might be considered 'non-Christian' art. As Turner says of his experience with Francis Schaeffer, 'It was possible for a well-loved hymn to be bad art and a painting by an utter reprobate to be good art. By making truth the sole criterion, Christians had often diminished the importance of human endeavor in the arts, and in doing this had deprived themselves of a wealth of cultural experience.'[315]

So much of the 21st Century church is about music and its place - the 'worship wars' have been an internecine conflict that has had little to do with *worship* in its proper, broader definition, and more about what kinds of music certain people prefer. If we accept that true worship encompasses more than our musical preferences, then we allow for other artistic expressions concerning our relationship to God and to each other.

---

[314] Park, *Nonsense*, 30.
[315] Turner, *Imagine*, 12.

For our hypothetical failing church, then, success is not regarded in terms of numbers, or in adopting the forms used by the successful church on the industrial estate. It is about approaching worship and worship forms artfully, involving the creative gifts of different members of the congregation and engaging them in the great story of redemption.

Rebalancing: Redeeming Technology

Monsma posits that 'Technological activity is a form of cultural activity. It is thereby a way of fulfilling the cultural mandate, which is itself one way of living out the Great Commandment. Thus… technology is to be done as a form of service to our fellow human beings and to natural creation.'[316] How should our apparently successful, techno-sympathetic church on the industrial estate approach the technological wealth that it has at its disposal? How can it best employ it in such a way that does not lead to isolation, homogenization and dehumanization?

The answer is similar to that for the village church, namely to consider the qualitative over the quantitative. Is the technology being employed to ensure a crowd-pleasing atmosphere? Are people drawn to this church because of the quality of their discipleship and spiritual growth, or are they there because of a slick show? What investment is there on the part of the church to be part of the wider community? How are relationships between members of the congregation fostered? Marva Dawn asks, 'Television has trained people in our culture to be passive, to get lots of information that we can't or don't act upon. How will we overcome that in the Church - or will we simply hear

---

[316] Monsma, *Responsible*, 68.

these words today, say "That was interesting" and walk out the door without wanting to change?'[317]

Is this a church that is more concerned with the packaging over the content? As Drane observes,

> A constant concern with shaping and packaging things can actually become a strategy for ensuring that nothing fundamental is going to change, because those who are recruited to run ready-made programmes are often the very ones who, with appropriate encouragement, might have had the energy and insight to create the experimental forms of worship and witness that could be transformational in their own local circumstances - if only all their time and enthusiasm was not being sapped with trying to adapt other people's ideas.[318]

The key here is the concept of worship as a transformative experience - both for the members of the church and as they interact with the wider community. As Page says, 'Worship - joyful worship - should not be a mindless rave style blow-out. We are celebrating God, not partying the night away. There is a purpose to proceedings. There is meaning not madness.'[319]

These are, admittedly, all questions that are not exclusive to the technological church. However, since the over-reliance on technology is something that exacerbates these issues, it is important that the pro-technological church pays greater attention to them.

Rebalancing: Reconciling Congregations

There are some churches that seem split along the lines of the technological and non-technological. They attempt to

---

[317] Dawn, *Waste*, 176.
[318] Drane, *McDonaldization*, 45.
[319] Page, *Nonsense*, 48.

minimize conflict and maintain a form of church unity by, paradoxically, separating opposing groups. It is a reflection of the 'worship wars' that creates two separate services for those preferring the modern over the traditional and vice versa. This is unity in disunity - a contradiction that creates a schizophrenic church - one body with two distinct personalities. Is it possible that these two groups can be reconciled by a broad approach to the arts?

'The Church is summoned to be a provisional embodiment within the finite world of a type of human existence that truly mirrors the being-in-relatedness of God... It is little use bemoaning the atrocious failures of the Church if we do not at the same time recognize its high cultural calling, not least in the arena of the arts.'[320]

Because much of our understanding of the aesthetic stems from the thinking of Kant and Descartes, we have separated our objective reasoning from our subjective emotion. 'I think therefore I am' places the seat of being squarely in the realm of the intellect and in many churches, the pinnacle of the service is the Word, the reading and exposition of Scripture. While this is undoubtedly vital, along with our songs and our prayers, the world of the senses, as we have already noted, seems confined to the voice.

Consequently, our sense of the artistic within our corporate worship has become stunted. Even where churches attempt to include dance, drama or visual art, it is often a token gesture and can be extremely hit-or-miss in terms of quality and our aesthetic judgments are made on a technical basis - we assess musicians on how fast they can play or how accurate they are or on how perfect their technique. This, we know, is a hallmark of

---

[320] Begbie, *Voicing*, 223.

McDonaldization - it is art made calculable, efficient, controllable and predictable. Conversely, if we base all our artistic decisions on how objects make us feel, then our worship becomes based around the subjective tastes of a few controlling individuals. We expect others to agree with what we perceive as the true definition of beauty. This is nothing short of cultural imperialism - the imposition of the 'superior' taste upon the lesser 'uneducated.'[321]

In order to be truly inclusive, we have to accept that other cultures, both generational and geographical, have tastes and practices other than our own. It is not up to us to bring them into our fold, but to 'prefer the other' in Christian love and acceptance, while at the same time remaining discerning and discriminating in ensuring that what is presented to the congregation is an appropriate response to the ultimate beauty of the glory of God. 'A Christian worship leader in middle age may find some type of nominally secular music to be enjoyable but incongruous in worship. Yet a young person may perceive different features of the style in question, or enjoy them differently, and therefore judge that the style of music could be spiritually enlivening and potentially worshipful.'[322]

From the point of view of the technophobe and the technophile, this is an acknowledgement that each group brings something that could be considered worshipful and potentially transformative. But it also needs awareness that in allowing either group to dominate shapes what we are able to say and not say about the nature of God and our relationship to him and to each other. If the technological church focuses on atmosphere and an emotional response through music, then it must be held in balance with the

---

[321] Burch Brown, *Taste*, 169.
[322] Ibid., 179.

non-technological that promotes the intellect and a slower, considered response. If the technological prizes scientific precision and accuracy, it must be checked with the non-technological sense of unquantifiable transcendence and awe. The truly aesthetic will be both intellectually, emotionally and, from the Christian perspective, spiritually engaging. It will also be fit for purpose.

Wolterstorff believes that 'Works of art are instruments by which we perform such diverse actions as praising our great men and expressing our grief, evoking emotion and communicating knowledge.'[323] But questions of artistic worth should not be reduced solely to ones of use, commercial or otherwise.[324] True artistry must surely engage the whole being, have an element of craftsmanship and technical expertise, and within the context of the church, be part of a deep and sustained encounter with God. It forms part of an overall journey from our point of origin, through meaningful acts as a community of worshipers, to a place of transformation from having been in God's presence.[325]

To be biblically faithful, then, we must acknowledge that we are beings of flesh and blood, spirit and mind, interacting and unified. When we separate these elements of our being, and separate our congregations along similar lines, we become less than we ought to be - unable to relate to ourselves, each other and even to God. *This* we relate to intellectually, *that* we relate to emotionally, never considering that we must relate to both *this* and *that* with our whole being.

---

[323] Wolterstorff, *Action*, 4.
[324] Begbie, *Voicing*, 6.
[325] Cherry, *Architect*, 17.

In the beginning, God created - and that creative process is carried on by God through his creation.[326] As beings created in the image of God, we have the opportunity to carry on in God's creativity by being creative ourselves. But we also have a responsibility to be creative, according to his will, in such a way that fulfils his purposes for the whole of creation. Our creativity is, at its heart, missional, and carries on in our day to day lives, as our reasonable service (Rom 12:1-2) bringing daily glory to God and declaring his continuing creative action in the world.[327]

So how does this help us to reconcile the 'traditional' and 'modern'? The technophile and the technophobe? Real art, real beauty, transcends this kind of division. It is a strongly unifying force which, counter-intuitively, grows stronger with greater diversity: 'The vital power of an imaginative work demands a diversity within its unity; and the stronger the diversity, the more massive the unity… A creative work in which all the characters automatically reproduce a single aspect of the writer's [or other artist's] mind is a work lacking in creative power.'[328]

New and old can co-exist in a corporate expression of worship that embraces what Huebner terms 'the "moreness" of life.'[329] It is a church that can echo Giorgio Vasari who recognizes that, 'The fact is that, other things being equal, modern works of art are just as fine as antiques; and there is no greater vanity than to value things for what they are called than for what they are.'[330]

This will not come without some sacrifice. Some churches, both technophile and technophobe, have allied themselves

---

[326] Phenix, *Education*, 87.

[327] Brand & Chaplin, *Art*, 72.

[328] Sayers, *Mind*, 41.

[329] Huebner, ' Spirituality,' 164.

[330] Vasari, *Lives*, 334.

to entertainment rather than to 'the quest for profound experience.'[331] Our failing village church did just that - in seeking to attract people it sought to entertain rather than to be transformed. In endeavouring to make themselves part of the world - to be 'relevant' - they lost the sense that they should, to an extent, stand apart from it. In providing deep, sustained encounter with God through a truly aesthetic experience that employs multiple art forms, the church can provide a stability and solidity that many people crave. In shifting the focus away from music and the voice, they can provide love and acceptance for people of all kinds - those who love modern music and those who do not, those who can sing or speak and those who cannot. In creating technological balance, the church has an opportunity, through artistic expressiveness, to communicate timeless and lasting truths to a society crying out for an anchor. But in a world where people feel unable to spare the time, a programmatic approach to corporate worship, reduced to a strict time limit, does little to help. If we are to contemplate and engage with God through art in any deep sense, we must not only consider our over-use of music, but also our relationship with the clock.[332]

According to P.T. Forsyth, 'The possibility of art...depends on a people's idea of God... Art depends on Religion... Our Religion depends on our thought of God. One way of thinking about God makes Art impossible, another makes it inevitable.'[333] In other words, our understanding of ourselves in relation to God determines what, or whether, we create. What, then, does it say of our

---

[331] Reimer, 'Music.'

[332] There is already a 'slow church' movement seeking to resist the forces of McDonaldization. Taking its lead from networks like Cittaslow, it seeks to get people to 'pay attention to the need for deliberate spiritual development.' Visit www.cittaslow.org and www.patheos.com/blogs/slowchurch/about/ for more information. See also Smietana, 'Slow.'

[333] Forsyth as quoted in Fuller, *Theoria*, 145.

relationship to and with God if we are not artful in our worship?

If we posit a technological solution to issues of technology within corporate worship then all we are doing is substituting one problem for another. Instead, technology as part of modern existence must be held in balance with a biblical understanding of how we are to relate to each other and to God. Increased artfulness makes that possible since it allows us to express the fullness of those relationships.

If we continue in a limited understanding of corporate worship, and fail to introduce a more artful expressiveness, continuing to reduce it to little more than a few songs on a Sunday, the spiritual life of believers will become utterly impoverished. Rather than the properly developed bodies that Paul desires in 1 Corinthians - metaphorically incorporating all the senses - we will carry on growing stunted, unbalanced and superficial disciples to the detriment, and by logical extension, to the ultimate destruction of the church.

Where do we go from here?

According to White, 'nearly every person who will participate in an act of Christian worship next Sunday morning will also be caught up in the experience of technologized living during the rest of the week.'[334] She rejects the notion that Christian worship equals 'good' while technology equals 'bad' and although we must continue to acknowledge the non-neutrality and value-ladenness of technology, we must also note the truth of White's assessment. She concludes that, 'if technology and worship can enter into a relationship of mutual critique,

---

[334] White, *Change*, 121.

there is the possibility that both may undergo genuine renewal.'[335]

Creative solutions, which the techno-sympathetic church cannot provide, are messy, inefficient, born out of relationship, in a specific context and through deep, invested and attentive spirituality. Christina Crook asks a question first posed by Albert Borgmann: 'What happens when technology moves beyond lifting genuine burdens and starts freeing us from burdens that we should not want to be rid of?' Her answer is that 'Instead of rejecting our limits, we must abide in them more fully, together holding firm to our humanity with the strength of a giant.'[336] In a similar way, churches must cling to humanity, celebrating the untidy, idiosyncratic and inefficient, revelling in creative imperfection instead of trying to smooth everything out into bland uniformity. Technology is efficient and effective, yes, but not representative of real experience.

Church leaders and congregations too afraid to make mistakes, at both ends of the technological spectrum, all too often opt for safety in conservatism. But this is counter-productive, 'A congregation so concerned not to cause offense that it manages to entertain and amuse but never to *worship God*... carries little credibility to a burned-out postmodern generation that rejects linear thought yet hungers for integrity of relationships.'[337]

David Toop says, 'Imagine the most likely use for the wired city of the future not in cyberpunk or megatropolising world music frameworks then, but as a high-tech campfire, people plugging in to remind themselves of life as it was when they were plugged out,

---

[335] White, *Change*, 122.
[336] Crook, 'Joy.'
[337] Carson, 'Worship', 60.

twisting their isolation into something resembling community.'[338] If technology creates 'something resembling community' then perhaps the church should think about creating *real* community. Unplugged, vibrant and genuinely creative instead of just virtually so. This is perhaps one of the biggest questions that churches must ask themselves in the 21st century: how do we move from online engagement with a technologically saturated world to create authentic, offline community?

We must seek to make the church the force that defines the culture of the age and transforms it, as it has done through history. This will require church leaders and congregations to invest significant amounts of time, money and prayer in their artists - particularly when the state is abrogating its responsibility for the arts. It will require them, above all, to take a risk. 'Imagination must be rediscovered as a seat for holy creativity. The body must be affirmed as the home for sacred sensuality and the worship of God…Spiritual life cannot be lived in a vacuum. People want to experience God through their emotions and senses.'[339]

This solution can and, indeed, must embrace and hold in balance both the technological and non-technological. As Malcolm Marshall puts it, 'Healthy and living tradition does not need to cut off the hand from the past which can nourish the present. Past and present must together reach out to the future.'[340]

---

[338] Toop, *Oceans*, 89.
[339] Detweiler, *Matrix*, 153.
[340] Marshall, *Renewal*, 68.

Join the debate:

Follow @davidmsnelling on Twitter
or visit facebook.com/Durotriges

BIBLIOGRAPHY AND FURTHER READING

Adams, D., 'How to Stop Worrying and Love the Internet,' *douglasadams.com* website, (August, 1999) (www.douglasadams.com).

Adorno, T., 'On The Fetish Character In Music and the Regression of Listening,' in J.M. Bernstein (ed.), *The Culture Industry: Selected Essays on Mass Culture*, London: Routledge, 1991.
—., *Aesthetic Theory*, London: Athlone Press, 1997.

Ananiadou, S., J McNaught & P. Thompson, *The English Language in the Digital Age,* Meta-Net White Paper Series, Springer, 2012.
(www.meta-net.eu/whitepapers).

Arthur, W.B., *The Nature of Technology*, London: Penguin Books, 2009.

Astley, J., T. Hone & M. Savage (eds.), *Creative Chords*, Leominster: Gracewing, 2000.

Bain, R., 'Technology and State Government', *American Sociological Review*, Vol. 2, No. 6 (Dec., 1937), pp. 860-874. (www.jstor.org).

Ball, P., *The Music Instinct*, London: Vintage Books, 2011.
—., 'Iamus, classical music's computer composer, live from Malaga,' *The Guardian* website, (1st July 2012) (www.theguardian.com/music).

BBC, 'Viewers prefer TV sets over mobile devices,' BBC website (17th February, 2014), (www.bbc.co.uk/news)

Begbie, J., *Voicing Creation's Praise*, London: T&T Clark, 1991.
—., *Theology, Music and Time*, Cambridge: Cambridge University Press, 2000.
—., *Resounding Truth*, London: SPCK, 2008.

Benjamin, W., *The Work of Art in the Age of Mechanical Reproduction*, London: Penguin Books, 1936.

Bingham, J., 'Social media killing off quiet reflection says Justin Welby,' *The Telegraph* website (17th June 2014) (www.telegraph.co.uk/finance).

Borgmann, A., *Technology and the Character of Contemporary Life*, Chicago: University of Chicago Press, 1987.

Bowater, C., *Creative Worship*, Basingstoke: Marshall, Morgan and Scott, 1986.

Braben, D.W. et al., 'We Need More Scientific Mavericks,' *Guardian.com* website, (18th March 2014) (www.theguardian.com/science).

Brand H. & A. Chaplin, *Art & Soul*, Downers Grove: IVP, 2001.

Brynjolfsson, E. & A. McAfee, *Race Against The Machine*, Lexington: Digital Frontier Press, 2011.

Burch Brown, F., *Good Taste, Bad Taste, Christian Taste*, Oxford: Oxford University Press, 2000.
—., *Inclusive Yet Discerning*, Grand Rapids: Wm. B. Eerdmans, 2009.

Carson D.A., 'Worship under the Word' in D. Carson (ed.), *Worship by the Book*, Grand Rapids: Zondervan, 2002.
—., *Christ and Culture Revisited*, Nottingham: Apollos, 2008.

Cherry, C., *The Worship Architect*, Grand Rapids: Baker Academic, 2010.

Connelly, C., 'Switched-on world is killing creativity, expert warns,' *news.com.au* website (28 May 2011) (www.news.com.au/technology).

Crook, C., 'The Joy of Missing Out: Finding Balance in a Wired World,' *secondnaturejournal.com* website (9th March 2015) (secondnaturejournal.com).

Dawn, M., *Reaching Out Without Dumbing Down*, Grand Rapids: Wm. B. Eerdmans, 1995.
—., *A Royal "Waste" of Time*, Grand Rapids: Wm. B. Eerdmans, 1999.

Demers, J., *Listening Through the Noise*, Oxford: Oxford University Press, 2010.

Detweiler C. & B. Taylor, *A Matrix of Meanings*, Grand Rapids: Baker Academic, 2003.

Drane, J., *The McDonaldization of the Church*, London: DLT, 2000.

Draper, B., *Thinking Biblically About The iPod*, Bletchley: Scripture Union, 2007.

Dyrness, W., *Visual Faith,* Grand Rapids: Baker Academic, 2001.

Eisler, H. & T. Adorno, 'The Politics of Hearing,' in C. Cox & D. Warner (eds.), *Audio Culture: Readings in Modern Music*, New York: Continuum, 2004, 73-75.

Ellul, J., *The Technological Bluff (trans. Le Bluff Technologique)*, Grand Rapids: Wm. B Eerdmans, 1990.
—., *The Technological Society (trans. La Technique ou l'enjeu du ciècle)*, New York: Vintage Books, 1964.

Engel, P. & P. Basden (eds.), *Six Views On Exploring the Worship Spectrum*, Grand Rapids: Zondervan, 2004.

Ewing, T., 'John Cage's 4'33": The Festive Sound of a Defeated Simon Cowell,' *The Guardian* website (30 September 2010) (www.guardian.co.uk/media).

Fuller, P., *Theoria: Art and the Absence of Grace*, London: Chatto & Windus, 1988.

Gabrielsen, P., 'Why Your Brain Loves That Song,' *Science* website (11 April 2013) (news.sciencemag.org/sciencenow).

Gordon, T.D., *Why Johnny Can't Sing Hymns*, Phillipsburg: P&R Publishing, 2010.

Greenfield, S., *Tomorrow's People*, London: Penguin Books, 2003.

Grey, A., 'Can the Church of England attract young people again,' *On Religion* website, (16th February 2015) (http://www.onreligion.co.uk).

Griffiths, P., *A Concise History of Western Music*, Cambridge: Cambridge University Press, 2006.

—., *Modern Music and After*, Oxford: Oxford University Press, 2010.

Groothius, D., *Truth Decay*, Downers Grove: IVP, 2000.

Harvey, J., 'Sketches for Mortuos Plango, Vivos Voco,' *BBC website*, (2005) (www.bbc.co.uk/radio3).

Hill, A., *Enter His Courts With Praise*, Eastbourne: Kingsway, 1993.

Hipps, S., *The Hidden Power of Electronic Culture*, Grand Rapids: Zondervan, 2005.
—., *Flickering Pixels*, Grand Rapids: Zondervan, 2009.

Huebner, D., 'Spirituality and Knowing,' in E. Eisner (ed.), *Learning and Teaching The Ways of Knowing*, Chicago: University of Chicago Press, 1985.

Hughes, R., *The Shock of the New*, New York: McGraw-Hill Inc., 1991.

Huxley, A., *Brave New World*, London: Vintage Books, 2007.

Inman, P. & A. Monaghan, 'Would Carlos Slim's Three-Day Working Week Actually Be Workable?' *Guardian.com* website (23rd July 2014) (www.theguardian.com/business).

Jones, J., 'Flat, Soulless and Stupid: Why photographs don't work in art galleries,' *The Guardian* website, (13th November 2014) (www.theguardian.com/artanddesign).

Jones, S., 'Rage Against Cowell Fuels Battle for Christmas No. 1,' *The Guardian* website (15th December 2009) (www.guardian.co.uk/music).

Kandinsky, W., *Concerning the Spiritual in Art*, New York: Dover Publications, 1977.

Katz, M., *Capturing Sound: How Technology Has Changed Music*, Berkeley: University of California Press, 2010.

Kimball, D., *Emerging Worship*, Grand Rapids: Zondervan, 2004.

Langer, S.K., *Feeling and Form*, New York: Charles Scribner's Sons, 1953.
—., *Philosophy In A New Key*, Boston: Harvard University Press, 2009.
—. *Problems of Art*, New York: Charles Scribner's Sons, 1957.

Liesch, B., *The New Worship*, Grand Rapids: Baker Books, 2001.

Maries, A., *One Heart, One Voice*, London: Hodder and Stoughton, 1985.

Marshall, M., *Renewal in Worship*, London: Marshall, Morgan and Scott, 1982.

Mathieu, W., *The Listening Book*, Boston: Shambhala Publications, 1991.

McLuhan, M., *Understanding Media*, London: Abacus, 1974.

McManus, J., 'Susan Boyle's Defiant "Dream",' *Washington Post* website, (16th April 2009) (www.washingtonpost.com).

Meyer, L., *Emotion and Meaning in Music*, Chicago: University of Chicago Press, 1956.

Monsma, S. et al (eds.), *Responsible Technology*, Grand Rapids: Wm. B. Eerdmans, 1986.

Moynagh, M., *Changing World, Changing Church*, London: Monarch Books, 2001.

Mumford, L., *Technics and Civilisation*, Chicago: University of Chicago Press, 1934.

Münch, 'McDonaldized Culture: The End of Communication?' in B. Smart (ed.), *Resisting McDonaldization*, London: SAGE Publications, 1999, 135-147.

Nicol, J., 'The lifecycle of a worship song (and why it matters for your church),' *Musicademy* website (13 February 2013) (www.musicademy.com).

Niebuhr H.R., *Christ and Culture*, New York: HarperOne, 1951.

Nyman, M., *Experimental Music*, Cambridge: Cambridge University Press, 1999.

Page, N., *And Now Let's Move Into A Time of Nonsense*, Milton Keynes: Authentic Media, 2004.

Percino, G., P. Klimek & S. Thurner, 'Instrumentational Complexity of Music Genres and Why Simplicity Sells,' *PlosOne* website, (31st December, 2014) (journals.plos.org).

Peterson, D., *Engaging With God*, Downers Grove: IVP Academic, 1992.
—., *Encountering God Together*, Phillipsburg: P&R Publishing, 2013.

Petridis, A., 'Steve Reich on Schoenberg, Coltrane and Radiohead,' *The Guardian* website (1 March 2013) (www.guardian.co.uk/music).

Phenix, P., *Education and the Worship of God*, Philadelphia: The Westminster Press, 1966.

Philips, C., 'Milli Vanilli's Grammy Rescinded by Academy: Music Organization revokes an award for the first time after revelation that the duo never sang on album,' *LA Times* website (20 November 1990) (articles.latimes.com/1990-11-20).

Philips, C., 'It's True: Milli Vanilli Didn't Sing: Duo could be stripped of its Grammy after admitting it lip-synced the best-selling "Girl You Know It's True.",' *LA Times* website (16 November 1990) (articles.latimes.com/1990-11-16).

Pinker, S., 'Why face-to-face contact matters in our digital age,' *The Guardian* website (20th March 2015) (www.theguardian.com/books).

Plato, *Phaedrus (trans. By Benjamin Jowett)*, Project Gutenburg Ebook edition, 2008.

Pope John Paul II, 'Letter of His Holiness Pope John Paul II To Artists,' *Vatican* website (23 April 1999) (www.vatican.va).

Postman, N., *Amusing Ourselves to Death*, York: Methuen, 1987.
—., *Technopoly*, New York: Vintage Books, 1992.

Reimer, B., 'Why Do Humans Value Music,' *NAFME* website (June 2012) (musiced.nafme.org).

Rienstra, D. & R. Rienstra, *Worship Words*, Grand Rapids: Baker Academic, 2009.

Ritzer, G., *The McDonaldization of Society (20th Anniversary edition)*, London: SAGE Publications, 2013.

Ross, A., *Listen to This*, London: Fourth Estate, 2011.
—., *The Rest Is Noise*, London: Fourth Estate, 2012.

Russell, B., 'In Praise of Idleness,' *An Anarchist Reading List* website,(1932) (www.zpub.com/notes/idle.html).

Sayers, D., *Mind of the Maker*, London: Mowbray, 1994.

Schmidt, C.J., *Sent and Gathered*, Grand Rapids: Baker Academic, 2009.

Scruton, R., 'Soul Music,' *The American* website (27 February 2010) (www.american.com).
—., *The Aesthetics of Music*, New York: Oxford University Press, 1997.
—., *Gentle Regrets*, London: Continuum, 2005.
—., *Modern Culture*, London: Bloomsbury, 2005.

Sedghi, A., 'Facebook: 10 years of social networking in numbers,' *The Guardian* website, (4th February 2014) (www.theguardian.com/news).

Shafer, R.M., 'The Music of the Environment,' in C. Cox & D. Warner (eds.), *Audio Culture: Readings in Modern Music*, New York: Continuum, 2004, 29-39.

Shriver, J., 'Milli Vanilli frontman says duo were musical "scapegoats",' *USA Today* website (28 January 2010) (usatoday30.usatoday.com/life).

Simpson, D., 'Riot In Steel City,' *The Guardian* website (28 November 2008) (www.guardian.co.uk/music).

Slouka, M., 'Listening for Silence: Notes on the Aural Life,' in C. Cox & D. Warner (eds.), *Audio Culture: Readings in Modern Music*, New York: Continuum, 2004, 40-47.

Smietana, R., '"Slow Church"'Movement Fights "McDonaldization" Of Worship, Says No "Fast Food" Way To Salvation' *Huffington Post* website (30th March 2014) (www.huffingtonpost.com).

Spinks, B., *The Worship Mall*, London: SPCK, 2010.

Starner, M., '5 Ways to Use Technology At Church,' *Matthew Starner* website (17 January 2012) (matthewstarner.com).

Stenovec, T., 'Facebook is now bigger than the largest country on Earth,' *Huffington Post* website, (28th January 2015) (www.huffingtonpost.com).

Stetzer, E., 'Why your church should be on social media right now,' *Christianity Today* website (10th February 2015) (http://www.christianitytoday.com/edstetzer).

Sweet, L., *Post-Modern Pilgrims*, Nashville: B&H Publishing, 2000.
—., *Carpe Mañana*, Grand Rapids: Zondervan, 2001.

Toop, D., *Ocean of Sound*, London: Serpent's Tail, 1995.

Townley, C., *Designing Worship Teams*, Nashville: Abingdon Press, 2002.

Turner, S., *Imagine: A Vision For Christians and the Arts*, Leicester: IVP, 2001.

Tyndale: the magazine, 'Church and Technology: A Survey of Ontario Churches,' *Tyndale University College & Seminary* website (Fall/Winter 2011/12) (www.tyndale.ca).

Vasari, G., *Lives of The Artists Volume I*, London: Penguin, 1965.

Viladesau, R., *Theology and the Arts,* New York: Paulist Press, 2000.

Ward, P., *Selling Worship*, Milton Keynes: Paternoster Press, 2005.

Warman, M., 'Technology and Data: the trends changing the world,' *The Telegraph* website, (12th July 2014) (www.telegraph.co.uk/technology).

Webber, R., *Ancient-Future Worship*, Grand Rapids: Baker Books, 2008.

Weinstein D. & M.A. Weinstein, 'McDonaldization Enframed,' in B. Smart (ed.), *Resisting McDonaldization*, London: SAGE Publications, 1999.

White, J., *Introduction to Christian Worship (3rd edition)*, Nashville: Abingdon Press, 2000.

White, S., *Christian Worship and Technological Change,* Nashville: Abingdon Press, 1994.

Williamson, S., 'Is Modern Worship Sort of Like A Cocaine Rush?' *Beliefs of the Heart* website (7 August 2012) (beliefsoftheheart.com).

Wilson-Dickson, A., *A Brief History of Christian Music*, Oxford: Lion Publishing, 1992.

Wolchover, N., 'Pop music all sounds the same nowadays,' *Live Science* website (27 July 2012) (www.livescience.com).

Wolterstorff, N., *Art In Action*, Carlisle: Solway Cultural Classics, 1997.

Made in the USA
Middletown, DE
28 January 2023